11+ COMPREHENSION PRACTICE PAPERS

Model Answers & In-Depth Guided Explanations

R. P. DAVIS

Copyright © 2020 Accolade Tuition Ltd
Published by Accolade Tuition Ltd
71-75 Shelton Street
Covent Garden
London WC2H 9JQ
www.accoladetuition.com
info@accoladetuition.com

The right of R. P. Davis to be identified as the author of this work has been asserted by him in accordance with the Copyright, Designs and Patents Act 1988.

All rights reserved. No part of this book may be reproduced in any form or by any electronic or mechanical means, including information storage and retrieval systems, without written permission from the author, except for the use of brief quotations in a book review.

ISBN 978-1-9163735-8-7

FIRST EDITION
1 3 5 7 9 10 8 6 4 2

Contents

Foreword

When sitting 11+ comprehension exams at top schools (be they independent power-houses, or high-flying grammars) you will notice that, although all of their papers follow the basic formula – an extract accompanied by a set of questions – the *types* of questions they ask can vary greatly. The reason for this is simple enough: a considerable number of these schools write their papers in-house, and that means you find quirks in some papers that you don't in others. Even papers produced by examining bodies, such as the ISEB, have their idiosyncrasies. And yet, for all these quirks, there is still a *huge* degree of overlap between these various papers, because ultimately these schools are all looking for a similar set of skills.

As a result, preparing for these exams is eminently possible. We simply need to identify the various types of questions that appear (including those quirky ones!), then hone the skills required to answer them.

The intention of this guide is not simply to show you what these exams tend to look like (although, as you work through it, you will inevitably get a sense of this nonetheless!). No, the intention is to go a step further, and show you how to decode the sorts of questions these 11+ comprehension papers tend to ask, and what "perfect" answers to these questions look like. Moreover, it also seeks to explain, *in detail*, how exactly the model answers provided satisfy the examiners' criteria, making it as easy as possible for students to understand how to emulate these answers.

You will notice, also, that there are a number of questions for which I have supplied alternative answers. This is because, when it comes to comprehension papers, there are frequently instances where there is not *one* correct answer – instead, there are a number of potential answers that might be worthy of scoring the marks. The alternative answers are therefore included to demonstrate how there is, very often, room for flexibility and creativity.

Now, before I press on, I feel it is important to make one crucial thing clear: this guide is explicitly aimed at those students looking to achieve at the very highest level. Many times in this guide I use sophisticated vocabulary and ideas. I promise you that my intention is *not* to intimidate. Rather, we must remember that these are competitive exams, and that the grading is administered by human beings – so it is imperative that we dazzle these examiners, and give them no choice but to fork over the marks!

Rest assured, however, that when I use these tricky words or phrases, I explain them as I go. As a result, by the time you finish working through this guide, you should have a whole new arsenal of words and phrases to help you attack papers of any kind!

How This Book Is Set Out

As mentioned, 11+ papers are incredibly varied. However, if you spend enough time and energy looking through past papers, you start to figure out what makes them tick, and notice certain patterns that emerge time and again. This book contains eight papers that have been split into four different "styles" of questioning – two papers for each style. I have labelled the four types of papers as follows:

1. The All Rounder Paper
2. The Close Language Paper
3. The Line By Line Paper
4. The Speculative & Creative Paper

The labels I've given each style should give you some indication of what the papers entail. It may well be the case that some of the 11+ comprehension papers you end up taking fit neatly into the one of these styles. However, it is just as possible that they wind up being a blend of two (or more) styles – after all, schools often tweak the style of paper they put out year on year. At any rate, I can assert with confidence that, if you are well versed in all four styles, you will have your bases covered, and be prepared for most anything.

The questions for each paper appear twice. The first time they will appear is immediately after the extract, so that students can, if they wish, have a go at tackling the paper. They will then appear a second time, but this time accompanied by model answers and detailed guidance.

Each of the papers includes a "time guide" – that is, the amount of time one would expect to be given to complete the paper in an exam hall. If students wish to complete some of these papers as practice, I suspect this may prove useful.

Insofar as difficulty is concerned, the first paper in each style might be described as "hard," and the second "devilish." Again, I feel the need to reiterate that my intention is *not* to intimidate. On the contrary, by exposing students to the reality of what is in store, I believe it ensures that, when it actually comes to entering the exam hall, you feel far more at ease.

There is no *correct* way to use this guide. Some students will feel comfortable working through it by themselves, whereas some may prefer to have a parent at hand to act as a kind of surrogate tutor. In any case, the intention of this book is to give the reader the experience of having an experienced tutor at their beck and call.

Exam Tips

Within this book, you will find a good deal of question specific advice. However, there are a number of more general tips that it is important for any 11+ candidate to keep in mind:

- When reading the extract, don't rush. Some papers even set aside 10 minutes explicitly for reading the paper, and do not allow you to look at the questions until those 10 minutes have elapsed. This does not mean that 10 minutes is always necessary – but keep in mind that every school will expect you to read the passage very carefully.
- Read the questions carefully. It sounds obvious, I know, but you wouldn't believe how many times I have seen bright students lose marks simply because they have misread the question
- Always write in full sentences, unless you are explicitly told this is not required.
- If you are unhappy with an answer, and feel as though you must write something else, do not cross out your old answer until you have fully finished writing the new one – you may be throwing away precious marks!
- Keep quotes from the text short (unless explicitly told otherwise). As a rule of thumb, try and ensure that your quotes are no more than six or seven words in length, and preferably shorter.
- Most papers tell you how many marks a question is worth. Keep this in mind when working out how much time to spend on any given question.
- Remember: just because a question is, for instance, worth three marks, that does not necessarily mean you need to give three separate points. Of course there *are* occasions when three marks require three points, and I shall discuss those occasions in this book – but this is not *always* the case.
- Many 11+ papers give candidates blank lines on which to compose their

answers. When these appear, take them seriously: they are guidelines regarding how long the examiners would like your answer to be.

Personal Note

When I talk about my academic career, I usually talk about my time spent at university: I studied English Literature & Language at UCL, then took a Masters at Cambridge University. However, a mere twenty years ago, I was in the same position that many of my readers find themselves in: eager to win a place at a top secondary school, and faced with a litany of exams. Of course, the exams have changed a fair bit since then; but what I'm trying to say is, not only have I been teaching 11+ students for many years, but I've also had firsthand experience of it – I know what it's like to live through!

Even though I now look back on that time through a rosy lens – I was offered places at all the top London private and grammar schools I sat for – I won't pretend as though it was not at times intimidating. However, I would observe that many parts of the 11+ English exams, including many questions in the comprehension papers, offer rare opportunities not just to jump through hoops, but to exercise your powers of creativity. That is not to say that these exam are *fun* – my memory of them is pretty much the exact opposite – but still, it is important to at least try and embrace this creative element and enjoy the challenge.

All Rounder Papers

Note: This type of paper does not focus on one or two particular skills. Rather, the questions it asks tend to be varied, and require you to demonstrate a range of skills. You will find questions that require you to deduce information; questions that ask you to explain things in your own words; and questions that require mini-essays.

Both of the All Rounder papers I've included here are out of a total of fifty marks.

So you can see what a typical 11+ comprehension paper looks like, the questions to the first paper you encounter in this guide will be accompanied by lines on which you can write your answers (that is, before you reach my model answers & guidance). However, for the sake of brevity, the other seven papers in this guide do not feature such lines.

Paper One: The Strange Case of Dr Jekyll and Mr Hyde

ALL ROUNDER PAPER; DIFFICULT; 40 MINUTES

In this passage, taken from a novel set in Victorian London, the lawyer Mr Utterson loiters on the street, hoping to encounter Mr Hyde.

1 It was a fine dry night; frost in the air; the streets as clean as a ballroom floor; the lamps, unshaken by any wind, drawing a regular pattern of light and shadow. By ten o'clock, when the shops were closed, the by-street was very solitary and, in spite of the low growl of London from all round, very silent. Small sounds carried far;
5 domestic sounds out of the houses were clearly audible on either side of the roadway; and the rumour of the approach of any passenger preceded him by a long time. Mr. Utterson had been some minutes at his post, when he was aware of an odd light foot-step drawing near. In the course of his nightly patrols, he had long grown accustomed to the quaint effect with which the footfalls of a single person, while he is still a great
10 way off, suddenly spring out distinct from the vast hum and clatter of the city. Yet his attention had never before been so sharply and decisively arrested; and it was with a strong, superstitious prevision of success that he withdrew into the entry of the court.

The steps drew swiftly nearer, and swelled out suddenly louder as they turned the end of the street. The lawyer, looking forth from the entry, could soon see what manner
15 of man he had to deal with. He was small and very plainly dressed and the look of him, even at that distance, went somehow strongly against the watcher's inclination. But he made straight for the door, crossing the roadway to save time; and as he came, he drew a key from his pocket like one approaching home.

Mr. Utterson stepped out and touched him on the shoulder as he passed. "Mr. Hyde,
20 I think?"

Mr. Hyde shrank back with a hissing intake of the breath. But his fear was only momentary; and though he did not look the lawyer in the face, he answered coolly enough: "That is my name. What do you want?"

"I see you are going in," returned the lawyer. "I am an old friend of Dr. Jekyll's—Mr.
25 Utterson of Gaunt Street—you must have heard of my name; and meeting you so conveniently, I thought you might admit me."

"You will not find Dr. Jekyll; he is from home," replied Mr. Hyde, blowing in the key. And then suddenly, but still without looking up, "How did you know me?" he asked.

"On your side," said Mr. Utterson "will you do me a favour?"

30 "With pleasure," replied the other. "What shall it be?"

"Will you let me see your face?" asked the lawyer.

Mr. Hyde appeared to hesitate, and then, as if upon some sudden reflection, fronted about with an air of defiance; and the pair stared at each other pretty fixedly for a few seconds.

35 "Now I shall know you again," said Mr. Utterson. "It may be useful."

"Yes," returned Mr. Hyde, "It is as well we have met; and *à propos*, you should have my address." And he gave a number of a street in Soho.

"Good God!" thought Mr. Utterson, "can he, too, have been thinking of the will?" But he kept his feelings to himself and only grunted in acknowledgment of the
40 address.

"And now," said the other, "how did you know me?"

"By description," was the reply.

"Whose description?"

"We have common friends," said Mr. Utterson.

45 "Common friends," echoed Mr. Hyde, a little hoarsely. "Who are they?"

"Jekyll, for instance," said the lawyer.

"He never told you," cried Mr. Hyde, with a flush of anger. "I did not think you would have lied."

"Come," said Mr. Utterson, "that is not fitting language."

50 The other snarled aloud into a savage laugh; and the next moment, with extraordinary quickness, he had unlocked the door and disappeared into the house.

The lawyer stood awhile when Mr. Hyde had left him, the picture of disquietude. Then he began slowly to mount the street, pausing every step or two and putting his hand to his brow like a man in mental perplexity.

An extract from Robert Louis Stevenson's *The Strange Case of Dr Jekyll and Mr Hyde*

---

1. On which road does Mr. Utterson claim to live? [2]

....

....

2. Explain the meaning of the words that follow with regards to how they appear in the text. [12]

a) Quaint (line 9)

....

b) Arrested (line 11)

....

c) Fronted (line 32)

....

d) Fixedly (line 33)

....

e) Disquietude (line 52)

....

f) Perplexity (line 54)

....

3. Identify the simile that appears in the extract's opening paragraph. [2]

....

....

....

4. Explain the effect of this simile. [2]

....

....

....

....

....

5. In your own words, explain how Mr. Utterson first came to realise that Mr Hyde might be approaching. [4]

....

....

....

....

....

....

....

....

....

6. "Good God!" thought Mr. Utterson, "can he, too, have been thinking of the will?" The quote above is an example of what literary technique? [2]

....

....

....

7. Re-read lines 13 to 23 ('The steps drew... what do you want'). Explain how the writer creates tension in this passage? Support your answer with evidence from these three paragraphs. [6]

....

....

....

....

....

....

....

....

....

....

....

....

8. Who do you think lives at the address outside of which Mr Utterson and Mr Hyde are talking? Use evidence from the text to support your answer. [3]

....

9. How does the writer create a sense of mystery in the final section of the story? (lines 47-54; '"He never told you".... mental perplexity.') [7]

10. What do you learn about the character of Mr Utterson? Write in as much detail as you can and include evidence to support your point. [10]

....

....

Paper One: Model Answers & Guidance

1. On which road does Mr. Utterson claim to live? [2]

Mr Utterson claims to live on Gaunt Street.

Many 11+ papers like to start off with a quick 'warm up' question that requires you to play the part of a detective. On this occasion, it is all about attention to detail: the answer is lurking in the text, and it is simply a case of combing through and teasing it out.

At line 12 Utterson introduces himself as 'Mr. Utterson of Gaunt Street.' Yes, there is some light inference required here – the question expects you to deduce that 'of Gaunt Street' is not some kind of aristocratic title. However, given that the exam paper is asking the question in the first place, and the fact that there is no other conceivable answer in the extract, we can confidently deduce that Gaunt Street is our answer.

Note that, although brief, my answer above constitutes a full sentence. As a rule of thumb, *always* write in full sentences unless you're explicitly told it is not necessary!

Note also that this paper has set aside two marks for this particular question. While it's certainly true that I've seen just as many 11+ papers that would only designate a single mark for a question like this, it is safe to assume – given the scope of the question – that we do not need to do anything more to secure both marks.

2. Explain the meaning of the words that follow with regards to how they appear in the text. [12]

a) Quaint (line 9)

Quaint here means pleasantly unusual.

b) Arrested (line 11)

Arrested here means piqued.

c) Fronted (line 32)

Fronted here means turned.

d) Fixedly (line 33)

Fixedly here means unwaveringly and intensely.

e) Disquietude (line 52)

Disquietude here means unease.

f) Perplexity (line 54)

Perplexity here means puzzlement or confoundment.

This style of question – that is, one that asks the candidate to give a definition of a word in light of its context – is a time-honoured favourite of 11+ examiners. In this paper, the candidate is presented with a list of words; however, other papers may ask for the definition of just one or two words.

Again, on this occasion, I am opting to use full sentences, since the exam paper has not given me permission to do otherwise.

When you are offering your definition, make sure you are using the same tense as the word you are defining. A good question to ask yourself is – would the word I'm using to define this fit seamlessly into the passage if I were to swap it in for the original word? If the answer is yes, you are on the right lines.

If you are uncertain of the meaning of any word, read the sentence within which it appears carefully – and, if need be, the sentences immediately preceding and proceeding it. In doing so, you might realise that you can make a decent educated guess. Remember, it is always better to make an educated guess than it is to leave it empty.

3. Identify the simile that appears in the extract's opening paragraph. [2]

The simile is as follows: '...the streets as clean as a ballroom floor.'

Students sometimes think that for a comparison to be a simile, the writer needs to have used the word 'like.' However, this is *not* the case: a simile can also be formulated using the word 'as' – such as in the example above.

Notice that I am not quoting the entire sentence. Rather, I'm quoting just the relevant snippet that contains the simile. The ellipsis (three dots) before the quote indicates that it appears mid-sentence.

4. Explain the effect of this simile. [2]

By likening the cleanness of the street to that of a ballroom floor – a space that is conventionally portrayed as architecturally clean and pristine, yet is also where drama and performance takes place – the writer establishes a visual image of an equally aesthetically clean and pristine street, while also tacitly hinting that it will play host to a performance of sorts.[1]

This is a tricky question, because the simile is not simply likening the street to a ballroom floor; rather, it is saying that a particular aspect of it – namely, its cleanness – is like a ballroom floor. Now, the word 'clean' can of course mean a number of different things. In the answer above, I have decided to focus on the idea of aesthetic cleanness; that is, the idea that the writer is presenting the street as being aesthetically simple and pristine.

As an aside, as you might have noticed, I am not holding back with my vocabulary. Please don't be intimidated by this. The fact of the matter is: the very top schools are looking for the best and the brightest – so building your vocabulary can only be a good thing. For the record, something's aesthetics are basically how they look. You will also notice that I've inserted a footnote in the answer. Footnotes such as this appear throughout the guide, and you can use them to look up explanations for words and phrases I've used.

There are two marks up for grabs here, and I'm confident that the detailed answer I've given – which focuses on the fact that the simile pivots on the idea of cleanness, but which has also gone the extra mile of pointing out that it hints at drama to come – has done enough to earn me both. However, if the question had been for 4 marks (and you can get questions of this kind that are indeed 4 marks) I would likely have made an extra observation to ensure I had all my bases covered. It would have looked something like this:

> **However, the word clean conjures a sense of not only pristine tidiness, but also of the street being uninhabited: clear of human life. As a result, by invoking the empty expanse of a ballroom floor, the writer emphasises just how uninhabited the street had been while Utterson was standing watch.**

5. In your own words, explain how Mr. Utterson first came to realise that Mr Hyde might be approaching. [4]

> **As a result of previous nights stalking this same backstreet, Utterson had trained his auditory powers to discern when someone was approaching: this individual's footsteps, as they approached, would become distinct from the background noise of the city, and grew increasingly more so as they came closer still.**[2]
>
> **On the night of this passage, Utterson was able to discern a pair of footsteps in the way outlined above, which told him someone was approaching. That it might have been Hyde is something Utterson seems to have been able to intuit from the unique patter of the footsteps, which triggers a gut instinct in Utterson – an uncanny sense that the person in question was likely to be Hyde.**[3]

Questions that ask you to put things 'in your own words' are another perennial favourite of 11+ question writers. The basic premise is that, if you are able to explain an element of the passage in your own words, you demonstrate that you truly understand it.

As the phraseology of the question implies, it's important to try as best you can to avoid the vocabulary used in the passage – you can see that my explanation, beyond the words 'footsteps' and 'distinct,' has been written with entirely fresh vocabulary.

Although there are four marks in play, when it comes to 'in your own words' questions, this does not mean you need to write four different things. Clarity is king; so while my answer is on the meaty side, I'm scoring those 4 marks chiefly through the accuracy and coherency of my answer.

6. "Good God!" thought Mr. Utterson, "can he, too, have been thinking of the will?" The quote above is an example of what literary technique? [2]

This technique is known as inner monologue.

We do not require two points in order to score both marks here. We simply need to have the right answer.

Unfortunately, for a question like this, you simply need to know the answer. My advice: make sure you brush up on literary techniques and technical terms in general. You will encounter more within this guide, which should help build up your knowledge base.

7. Re-read lines 13 to 23 ('The steps drew... what do you want'). Explain how the writer creates tension in this passage? Support your answer with evidence from these three paragraphs. [6]

A key method the writer uses to create tension is timing: although we are given the impression that Hyde is rapidly approaching – 'the steps drew swiftly nearer' – the reader is made to wait for the showdown: the writer slows the pace with long sentences and interpolated phrases, such as 'even at that distance'.[4] The phrase 'even at that distance' also suggests that Hyde, despite moving 'swiftly,' still remains some distance off, further creating tension through delay.

The free indirect third person style, which places the reader in Utterson's shoes, enhances the tension by vicariously exposing the reader to Utterson's uncertainty.[5] Until Utterson initiates conversation, he remains uncertain whether the individual is indeed Hyde. The reader feels Utterson's sense of Hyde being somehow unnerving ('the look of him' goes against Utterson's 'inclination') despite appearing 'plainly' dressed – Hyde's inexplicability itself a source of tension.[6] Tellingly, Utterson is described at one point merely as 'the watcher,' the removal of his name tacitly encouraging the reader to step into his shoes.

Finally, Hyde's disorientating personality creates tension. His extreme animalistic reaction – his 'hissing intake of breath' is almost serpentine – ensures that Hyde inspires unease even as he himself is feeling fear. Moreover, his radical mood swings – he is, next moment, answering

'Coolly enough' – is disorientating, and ensures Hyde induces tension through his unpredictability.

Right, there's plenty to say about the question and answer above.

First off, we're told that it's worth six marks; but since almost every top private school marks these papers internally, and publish no standardised mark schemes, it's impossible to know whether they want you to make two points or three.

I personally advocate a "cover all your bases" mentality: if you can think of three points, and you can back them all up, then you make it very tough for the examiner to withhold marks. That said, if you can only identify two points in the heat of the exam, but can argue them well, you may still find yourself scoring over four marks.

Another key thing to keep in mind when answering a question of this kind – that, a question that asks you to focus on a 'mini' passage within the extract – is to make sure you do not just focus on one part of this mini passage. You need to take the whole of the mini passage into account.

Now, let's look at the actual substance of my answer. The question asked me to *explain* – and it also gave me broad scope to use any kind of evidence I deemed appropriate. As a result, I ensured that my answer did not just look closely at the language used, but also at factors such as sentence length, pacing, and narrative techniques. In doing so, I demonstrated to the examiner an understanding that the writer uses a range of tools to realise his aims.

You'll also notice that I talk at one point about the 'free indirect third person.' I know this sounds like an intimidatingly technical phrase, but let me explain.

You may already know that a first person story is one written from a character's own point of view ('I went there. I did this'), and that a third person story is one in which a narrator describes the actions of the story's character's ('He did this. She did that'). But have you ever noticed how, when you are reading a third person story, it sometimes still feels as if you are subtly getting a certain character's distinct point of view? As if the narrator perhaps has a secret insight into that character's mind? Well, this is known as the 'free indirect third person;' and, while technically still a type of third person narration, it feels a bit like a blend between first person and third person.

Examiners like it when you have sophisticated technical vocabulary up your sleeve. I want you to be able to spot it when you see it, as I have done here.

Finally, I'd observe that questions relating to tension – e.g. *how does the writer create tension, or how does the writer make the passage tense*, and so forth – are fairly popular, so do make sure you feel ready to tackle questions of this kind.

8. Who do you think lives at the address outside of which Mr Utterson and Mr Hyde are talking? Use evidence from the text to support your answer. [3]

It would appear as though Mr Jekyll lives at the address. Our best clue is Hyde's assertion, when accosted by Utterson, that Utterson 'will not find Dr. Jekyll; he is from home.' Implicit here is that this address is Jekyll's home, and that Hyde has assumed that Utterson is there in the hopes of visiting Jekyll.[7]

This question – like the first one in this paper – once again requires you to play the sleuth. However, whereas the first question of this kind simply required you to spot the correct information, the answer to *this* question is never explicitly spelt out in the text. Instead, you need to be able to infer it by "reading between the lines," as I've done above.

9. How does the writer create a sense of mystery in the final section of the story? (lines 47-54; '"He never told you".... mental perplexity.' [7]

The writer creates mystery at the passage's close through Hyde's puzzling behaviour. His explosive refutation that Utterson had heard his name via Jekyll – '"He never told you," cried Mr. Hyde, with a flush of anger' – raises questions with regard not only to how Hyde can be so certain, but also to his seemingly disproportionate 'anger.' That Hyde's anger seems to strangely contort into a kind of subversive laugh – he 'snarled aloud into a savage laugh' – adds another layer of mystery: the reader is given little indication of what warrants this laughter.[8]

The writer also creates mystery through his use of staging and physical space. The way Hyde swiftly ducks indoors – he 'unlocked the door and disappeared' – deprives the reader of any glimpse inside, leaving one to speculate what curiosities may be unfolding within, while the word 'disappeared' almost seems to grant the manoeuvre the mystery of a magician's vanishing act. The total effect is akin to the lowering of the curtain at a cliff-hanger during a theatrical performance: a prompt that literally conceals, but also symbolically signposts a moment of mystery and suspense.[9]

Finally, Utterson's own sense that he is entangled in a mystery functions as a prompt to the reader, encouraging them to feel the same way. Utterson's physical demeanour, with 'his hand to his brow like a man in mental perplexity,' powerfully communicates the mystery he is

grappling with. Moreover, the strange circularity of the simile – Utterson, a man very obviously in mental perplexity, is likened to 'a man in mental perplexity' – again contributes to the sense of overwhelming mystery: the bafflement it induces is so extreme that similes short-circuit as they try and convey it.

Again, we have a question that, if we play our cards right, is worth a considerable number of marks. Again, it is asking us to focus on a mini passage. And although the word 'explain' is not explicitly used, we have another question that once again requires us to do just that (indeed, questions that ask us 'how' the writer achieves an effect are generally questions that require us to explain).

Given the time constraints, and the fact that the six mark question above was comfortably satisfied by an argument that was comprised of three points, it seems unlikely that the examiners are looking for four separate points to score the seven marks here. So, instead, I decided to put together an answer comprising of three points, and simply made sure to delve into each of them in plenty of detail.

Notice how, once again, I break things down into distinct ideas. Before I started writing, I wrote three quick bullet points:

- Hyde's mysterious behaviour
- Mystery created through staging
- Mystery implied through Utterson's reaction.

It is, if you like, a very brief essay plan, and it ensured that I knew where I was going when I started writing.

Also, when the mini passage contains a simile, it's always good to try and include it in your answer. I would argue that the simile in this mini passage was quite tricky; but, even then, I made an effort to offer an analysis that contributed meaningfully to my answer.

10. What do you learn about the character of Mr Utterson? Write in as much detail as you can and include evidence to support your point. [10]

What is established first and foremost is Utterson's capacity for patience and his attunement to detail. In the opening paragraph, the reader learns that Utterson's stake-out of this address is not a one-off affair; it is something he had done repeatedly over the course of multiple 'nightly patrols,' and, given the fact he had been 'some minutes at his post,' something that takes up considerable time on each occasion. That

Utterson is willing to stalk the streets in hopes of meeting Hyde indicates a strain of patience. Moreover, the auditory mechanism he devises to detect oncoming people, in which he listens out for the 'the rumour of the approach,' not only suggests patience (one would surmise it took time to perfect), but also an attunement to minutiae in his environment.[10]

Utterson appears to subscribe to an ethos of decorum during social exchanges.[11] **This is demonstrated by the superficial deference he exhibits when addressing Hyde: the comment, 'I thought you might admit me', appears to defer power to Hyde, and so too does Utterson's request to be granted a request: "will you do me a favour?"**[12] **However, his ethos of decorum is perhaps exemplified best when Utterson, in a bid to enforce decorum, reprimands Hyde for his words spoken in anger: 'That is not fitting language.'**

Yet while Utterson pays lip service to decorum, also evident in his character is a hypocrisy.[13] **Utterson may speak in a way that implies decorum, and demand that Hyde does too; however, his conduct in this passage – his 'nightly patrols,' the way he accosts Hyde from behind (he 'stepped out and touched him on the shoulder') – can hardly be considered 'fitting' or polite. On the contrary, they are invasive tactics that are directly at odds with the codes of decorum.**

Also evident in Utterson is a strain of verbal cunning, though it is a cunning that enjoys limited success. Although subtle, Utterson's evasive response to Hyde's request for information – "On your side... will you do me a favour?" – successfully allows him to play his cards close to his chest. Moreover, while one does not know whether Hyde's accusation that Utterson has lied is true, the notion that Utterson *might* have lied further casts him as a cunning character. However, if he had lied, the fact that he was caught in the act suggests that there are limits to his powers of cunning.

Questions of this kind – that is, "*what do you learn about the character of X?*" questions – are seen in comprehension papers from a number of top schools, though they sometimes appear with slightly different phrasing: for instance, "*what are your impressions of Character X?*"

The key thing here is not to simply start writing, but to take a moment to draw out a few distinct observations regarding the character in question. On this occasion, since 10 marks were in play, I made sure to use four points, since three would likely have been too few. I'm counting on the fact that each point will win me, at a minimum, two marks, and that a couple of my points are sophisticated enough, and written with sufficient flair, that the examiner will feel inclined to award them three points.

As with the previous question, I also made a mini plan before I started writing, which took the form of four brief bullet points:

- Patient & attuned to details
- Superficially subscribes to ideals of decorum
- Hypocritical in behaviour
- Verbally cunning

Because I had these four "themes," I knew exactly what I wanted to write. This tactic ensures you have direction and clarity as you set about writing.

You'll notice also that I always back my points up with quotes from the text. These quotes are rarely long – usually no more than about six or seven words – and they are almost always integrated into the flow of sentence. This is what you ought to be striving for! Simply dumping very long quotes into your work is unlikely to impress: they want to see that you have the ability to extract the most relevant material.

Paper Two: Three Soldiers

ALL ROUNDER PAPER; DEVILISH; 40 MINUTES

This is an extract from a novel set during World War One. Chrisfield is an American soldier, deployed in Europe. In this passage, he is surveying a forest for enemy troops.

---

1 As far as he could see in every direction were the grey trunks of beeches bright green with moss on one side. The ground was thick with last year's leaves that rustled maddeningly with every step. In front of him his eyes followed other patches of olive-drab moving among the tree trunks. Overhead, through the mottled light and dark
5 green of the leaves he could see now and then a patch of heavy grey sky, greyer than the silvery trunks that moved about him in every direction as he walked. He strained his eyes down each alley until they were dazzled by the reiteration of mottled grey and green. Now and then the rustling stopped ahead of him, and the olive-drab patches were still. Then, above the clamour of the blood in his ears, he could hear
10 batteries "pong, pong, pong" in the distance, and the woods ringing with a sound like hail as a heavy shell hurtled above the tree tops to end in a dull rumble miles away.

Chrisfield was soaked with sweat, but he could not feel his arms or legs. Every sense was concentrated in eyes and ears, and in the consciousness of his gun. Time and again he pictured himself taking sight at something grey that moved, and firing. His
15 forefinger itched to press the trigger. He would take aim very carefully, he told himself; he pictured a dab of grey starting up from behind a grey tree trunk, and the sharp detonation of his rifle, and the dab of grey rolling among the last year's leaves.

A branch carried his helmet off his head so that it rolled at his feet and bounced with a faint metallic sound against the root of a tree.

20 He was blinded by the sudden terror that seized him. His heart seemed to roll from side to side in his chest. He stood stiff, as if paralyzed for a moment before he could stoop and pick the helmet up. There was a curious taste of blood in his mouth.

"Ah'll pay 'em fer that," he muttered between clenched teeth.

His fingers were still trembling when he stooped to pick up the helmet, which he put
25 on again very carefully, fastening it with the strap under his chin. Furious anger had taken hold of him. The olive-drab patches ahead had moved forward again. He followed, looking eagerly to the right and the left, praying he might see something. In every direction were the silvery trunk of the beeches, each with a vivid green streak on one side. With every step the last year's russet leaves rustled underfoot, madden-
30 ingly loud.

Almost out of sight among the moving tree trunks was a log. It was not a log; it was a bunch of grey-green cloth. Without thinking Chrisfield strode towards it. The silver trunks of the beeches circled about him, waving jagged arms. It was a German lying full length among the leaves.

35 Chrisfield was furiously happy in the angry pumping of blood through his veins.

He could see the buttons on the back of the long coat of the German, and the red band on his cap.

He kicked the German. He could feel the ribs against his toes through the leather of his boot. He kicked again and again with all his might. The German rolled over heav-
40 ily. He had no face. Chrisfield felt the hatred suddenly ebb out of him. Where the face had been was a spongy mass of purple and yellow and red, half of which stuck to the russet leaves when the body rolled over. Large flies with bright shiny green bodies circled about it. In a brown clay-grimed hand was a revolver.

Chrisfield felt his spine go cold; the German had shot himself.

45 He ran off suddenly, breathlessly, to join the rest of the reconnoitering squad. The silent beeches whirled about him, waving gnarled boughs above his head. The German had shot himself. That was why he had no face.

Chrisfield fell into line behind the other men. The corporal waited for him.

"See anything?" he asked.

50 "Not a goddam thing," muttered Chrisfield almost inaudibly. The corporal went off to the head of the line. Chrisfield was alone again. The leaves rustled maddeningly loud underfoot.

An extract from John Dos Passos's *Three Soldiers*

1. What colour is the sky in this extract? [2]

2. Explain the meaning of the words that follow with regards to how they appear in the text. [12]

a) Mottled (line 4)

b) Rustling (line 8)

c) Consciousness (line 13)

d) Seized (line 20)

e) Ebb (line 40)

f) Gnarled (line 46)

3. What simile is used in the opening paragraph? [2]

4. Explain the effect of this simile. [2]

5. In your own words, explain why Chrisfied says ""Ah'll pay 'em fer that"' at line 23? [4]

6. The phrase ""pong, pong, pong" is an example of what literary technique? [2]

7. Re-read lines 24 to 34 ('His fingers were still trembling... full length among the leaves'). Explain how the writer creates tension in this passage? Support your answer with evidence from these two paragraphs. [6]

8. What colour uniforms are the reconnoitering squad dressed in? [3]

9. Look again at lines 38-44 (He kicked the German... had shot himself]. How does the writer make this portion of the story terrifying? [7]

10. What do you learn about the character of Chrisfield? Write in as much detail as you can and include evidence to support your point. [10]

Paper Two: Model Answers & Guidance

1. What colour is the sky in this extract? [2]

The colour of the sky is a heavy grey.

Again, this type of question is simply ensuring that you are paying attention to details. The colour of the sky is disclosed in the first paragraph, in the midst of a fairly long sentence. The examiners want to make sure you've spotted it.

2. Explain the meaning of the words that follow with regards to how they appear in the text. [12]

a) Mottled (line 4)

Mottled here means spotted or dotted.

b) Rustling (line 8)

Rustling here means gently crackling.

c) Consciousness (line 13)

Consciousness here means awareness.

d) Seized (line 20)

Seized here means accosted.

e) Ebb (line 40)

Ebb here means recede.

f) Gnarled (line 46)

Gnarled here means knotted and distorted.

3. What simile is used in the opening paragraph? [2]

The simile used is as follows: "...woods ringing with a sound like hail as a heavy shell hurtled above the tree tops."

Unlike in the previous paper, the simile you are being asked to extract here *does* contain the word 'like.' Notice how I use an ellipsis. I've done this because the sentence in which the simile appears is fairly long; so, to save time, I've used the ellipsis to cut off the first part of the sentence. However, I've made sure to leave in enough of the words that appear before the word 'like' to ensure that the quote still makes sense in isolation.

4. Explain the effect of this simile. [2]

'By likening the sound of the mortar shells to hail, the author conjures a sense of ubiquity: in the same way hail sounds as if it envelopes from all directions, so too does the sound of the shell give Chrisfield the sense of being enveloped.[1] Moreover, by likening the shell to the natural phenomenon of precipitation, the author is subtly saying that the shells now feel as natural to Chrisfield as hail falling from the sky.'

The potentially tricky thing with this simile is knowing what the word 'shell' means; however, one should be able to infer from the passage and the war setting that they are a kind of weapon.

My answer here is playing things safe. I would strongly expect the first sentence of my answer should be enough to secure both marks. However, just in case they are looking for two points, I have made a quick second observation.

That said, the effects of a simile are often manifold, which means that you could identify different qualities to the ones I have and still expect to score the marks. For instance, I could have focused on the destructive nature of hail instead:

> **'Given that hail, in contrast to rain, is solid, and, in contrast to snow, is hard as it falls, hail might be considered more physically punishing to the environment. As a result, by likening the sound of shells to hail, the author captures the way the shells punish and tear through the physical environment of the canopy, and Chrisfield is hearing the ringing report of this happening.'**

This time, I've focused instead on how the analogy to hail might suggest that the sound Chrisfied hears connotes destruction to the environment. However, the answer is clearly thought out and reasonable, so would also do the job.

5. In your own words, explain why Chrisfied says '"Ah'll pay 'em fer that"' at line 23? [4]

> **The "'em" to whom Chrisfield is referring, and to whom his threat is levelled, is the Germans. Chrisfield understands that it was a branch, not the Germans, that knocked off his helmet. However, Chrisfield here is not vowing to retaliate against the branch for knocking off his helmet; he is vowing to retaliate against the Germans for the discomfort and fear they have induced in him – a discomfort and fear that was particularly acute when he was picking up his helmet and feeling vulnerable.[2] As mentioned, the phrase "pay 'em" is a threat: he is threatening to get pay back against the enemy combatants.**

This particular *'in your own words'* question is arguably more tricky than your standard question of this variety, because it is asking you not only to put things in your own words, which is a challenge in its own right, but also to explain something that is not spelt out explicitly in the text.

The first two marks will be awarded if you can demonstrate that you understand that he is levelling these words at the enemy troops, and that it is for the feeling of vulnerability they have induced in him. The next mark is for acknowledging that his words constitute a threat. The fourth is for the coherency and sophistication of your answer

– have you explained these points in a flowing and eloquent way that can truly be described as your own words?

6. The phrase '"pong, pong, pong" is an example of what literary technique? [2]

This phrase is an example of onomatopoeia.[3]

This question does *not* require two separate points: they simply want you to demonstrate that you understand the literary technique in question, and that you are aware of the technical word that is used to describe it.

However, in all likelihood they would expect you to spell onomatopoeia correctly to pick up both marks. Given its consecutive vowels, it is a tricky word to spell; so it is definitely one to commit to memory.

7. Re-read lines 24 to 34 ('His fingers were still trembling... full length among the leaves'). Explain how the writer creates tension in this passage? Support your answer with evidence from these two paragraphs. [6]

A key vehicle by which the writer generates tension is through the conflict between Chrisfield's physical restraint and delicacy, and his psychological state of near overwhelming anger. The reader is informed that Chrisfield places the helmet back on his head 'very carefully,' the abundance of care further communicated by the focus on minutiae: he 'fasten[ed] it with the strap.'[4] However, he is internally in an explosive state: 'furious anger had taken hold of him.' The way this personified anger seems almost to be possessing him, encroaching on his agency, conjures further tension, for it suggests that Chrisfield's restraint may imminently give way to explosive action.[5]

Tension is also created through nature, which is presented not only as a menace in its own right, but also as the potential host and accessory to hidden threats. The 'vivid green streak' down the side of each tree creates an unnerving uniformity, whereas the rustling 'russet leaves' are not just unsettling, but also run the risk of alerting enemies to Chrisfield's whereabouts.[6] **Moreover, the way in which natural objects are confusable with potential threats – the German soldier is initially misidentified by Chrisfield as a log (it 'was a log. It was not a log') – further creates tension, since it indicates that the terrain is capable of concealing threats, and implies more may be lurking.**

Tension is also created through pacing. The writer uses various tactics

to delay the discovery of the German. Given that the rustling leaves had been mentioned prior to this particular passage, it is clear the reference is not only there for descriptive purposes; the additional sentence also delays the revelation, building suspense. Once Chrisfield has realised that what he has seen is *not* a log, but before he identifies what it truly is, the writer inserts yet another sentence, referencing 'the silver trunks of the beeches.' Again, while surely this is included in part to further depict the terrain as treacherous, it also functions to delay and conjure tension.

Six marks are up for grabs in this question. To play it safe, I decided to make three distinct points, ensuring that each point I included was detailed enough to secure at least two marks apiece.

As I have mentioned before, when presented with a question of this kind, I would *not* suggest just starting to write immediately. Instead, have a think about what you'd like to say, and put together an incredibly quick plan, so you can write with coherency and direction. I picked out three "themes" before starting, and wrote the following (very brief) bullet points for myself as prompts:

- Conflict between Chrisfield's stealth and anger.
- The terrain inspiring menace and hiding threats.
- Pacing and speed: the writer ekes out information.

At all times, the fact I've been asked to *explain* is at the front and centre of my mind, and I am continually making clear how the theme I've identified – be it the presentation of the terrain, or the pacing – is used to create tension. This is vital: it ensures that you are answering the question!

8. What colour uniforms are the reconnoitering squad dressed in? [3]

They are dressed in olive drab uniforms.

We have another sleuthing question here – the three marks are not set aside for three separate points, but quite simply for identifying the correct answer.

In short, many candidates will struggle to know what the writer is talking about when he intermittently references the 'patches of olive-drab.' Attentive students will deduce that they are the outlines of the other soldiers in Chrisfield's reconnoitering squad.

9. Look again at lines 38-44 (He kicked the German... had shot himself]. How does the writer make this portion of the story terrifying? [7]

A key way the writer induces terror is by using a free indirect style that allows events to be relayed from Chrisfield's point of view, and thus vicariously allows the reader to experience Chrisfield's emotional range. The first emotion the reader vicariously encounters is in fact *not* Chrisfield's horror, but his hatred, which sees him kick the German 'over and over.' However, the way it abruptly dissipates – 'the hatred suddenly ebb[ed] out of him' – leads to a emotional vacuum that makes the ensuing horror all the more harrowing.[7] Indeed, when the horror hits home, and Chrisfield feels 'his spine go cold,' his horror acts as a rubric for the reader, powerfully compelling them to feel an equivalent terror.[8]

The writer also induces terror through his visceral description of the deceased German.[9] Instead of simply referencing a bullet wound, the writer goes into grotesque detail: he references the 'spongy mass of purple and yellow and red' that has displaced the German's face; he obliquely evokes the moisture the corpse exudes, describing how the corpse became 'stuck to the russet leaves;' and he invokes the 'large flies with bright shiny green bodies' feeding on the corpse.[10] Such a detailed description of the corpse forces the reader to confront the brutal realities of war, and is horrifying in its own right.

The writer also employs an abrupt, matter-of-fact style that induces horror through shock tactics. The revelation that the German 'had no face' appears in an abrupt and shocking standalone sentence – this choice ensures that nothing detracts from its horrifying import. The writer uses almost an identical tactic when revealing that 'the German had shot himself.' Again, the writer spells the revelation out abruptly and matter-of-factly; again, the writer uses structure to ensure it shocks, for although it is not a standalone sentence, the fact it is alone after a semi-colon, and a key part of a single line paragraph, lends it a similar punch.

Again we have a question that asks us to focus on a passage within the extract. Again, although the word 'explain' is not explicitly used, the 'how does...' formulation indicates that we are indeed required to offer an explanation. Again, the seven marks in the context of a 'mini essay' type question points towards the need for at least three substantial points – each point earning at least two points, and an extra point to be earned through sophistication of ideas, quality of argument, and so forth.

True to form, before I started writing, I put together one of my very brief plans:

- The reader is encouraged to feel Chrisfield's own horror.
- Visceral description of the body.
- Shock tactics achieved through abrupt revelations.

Notice that I once again discuss the nature of the third person narration as part of my answer, and also invoke sentence length. As mentioned previously, the ability to discuss more than just the language used will impress.

10. What do you learn about the character of Chrisfield? Write in as much detail as you can and include evidence to support your point. [10]

Perhaps the most immediately apparent facet of Chrisfield's character is his capacity to concentrate, which is signified through his acute attunement to his surroundings. While the narrative is rendered in the third person, it is made clear that the litany of details – the beeches 'bright green with moss;' the 'patches of olive-drab;' the 'mottled light' – are the result of Chrisfield's personal observations (as opposed to the narrator's), since there are repeated references to Chrisfield engaging his sensory organs: 'his eyes followed;' 'he strained his eyes;' 'he could hear.' Moreover, that these observations are not casual, but the result of supreme concentration, is also made explicit when the reader is informed that Chrisfield's 'every sense was concentrated in eyes and ears.' The word 'concentrated' not only points to his laser focus in that moment, but also his broader capacity to concentrate.

Also apparent is that Chrisfied has been brutalised by war, and that this brutalisation has created a sadistic streak in him.[11] This sadism is powerfully conveyed when Chrisfied fantasises about shooting an enemy combatant. Aside from the fact that daydreaming about shooting at a German 'dab of grey' implicitly communicates a sadistic desire to do just that (it would, after all, be a literal dream come true), the reader is told more explicitly that Chrisfield's 'forefinger itched to press the trigger.' The word 'itch' implies not just a desire to punish the Germans, but a compulsion: he feels it is the only way he can be satisfied.

However, it is clear that this sadism does not exist in a vacuum; rather, Chrisfield has been made brutal by the war. This is best captured when he mutters that he'll 'pay 'em fer that.' This reveals that his sadistic joy at the idea of inflicting pain on the Germans is not arbitrary; it is, to his mind, payback for the suffering he has undergone at their hands.[12]

Although, at first, his discovery of the German corpse seems only to

confirm his sadistic streak – he finds joy ('furiously happy') in his anger, and kicks the body – the encounter ultimately reveals Chrisfield's striking capacity for empathy. That the anger 'ebbs' out of him when he realises the German had committed suicide is no coincidence: it marks Chrisfield's implicit realisation that the German combatant, rather than being a vicious tormentor, was also – like Chrisfield himself – a tormented soul. The degree to which this reverberates with his sense of empathy is not only captured in the harrowing refrain ('the German had shot himself') but also in the intensity with which he runs back to join his squad.[13]

Finally, one might note a hint of subversiveness in Chrisfield's character. In response to the corporal's request for an update, Chrisfield claims he saw 'not a goddam thing.' Aside from the fact he is lying to his superior, the word 'goddam,' a curse word in American parlance, hints at a burgeoning distaste for the corporal's authority.[14]

On this occasion, I was able to spot five relevant points:

> Capacity for concentration.

> Sadism.

> Brutalised by war.

> Capacity for empathy.

> A subversive streak.

However, I knew, insofar as timing was concerned, that it was unrealistic to try and tackle all five in depth. As a result, I decided that I would tackle three in great depth, and two (the third and fifth point) briefly. Even if the shorter points were to garner, say, three marks between them, I'd still feel comfortable with the prospect of scoring seven marks from my three more meaty points.

When asked about characters, it is important to read between the lines. Chrisfield's sadistic desire to hurt the Germans is pretty clear; however, the fact that he has been made brutal by the conditions of war is more subtle. Moreover, while his subversive streak is perhaps something we can intuit fairly easy, spelling out how we came to intuit it is perhaps a little more tricky.

Close Language Papers

Note: While the next two papers do share some similarities with the first two – again, we have short questions asking us to deduce things, spot details, and define certain words – the higher-scoring questions in this paper are inviting us to look closely at the writer's choice of language and to discuss these choices in explicit detail. In many respects, this style of paper is more focused: you do not need to write mini essays in quite the same way – rather, the name of the game is demonstrating your intimate understanding of individual quotations. Indeed, the questions themselves are often more detailed, frequently making it explicit what they wish to see from you.

Both of the Close Language papers I've included here are out of a total of forty marks.

Paper Three: Hard Times

CLOSE LANGUAGE PAPER; DIFFICULT; 40 MINUTES

This passage, set in Victorian England, starts with Thomas Gradgrind walking past a circus at the edge of town.

---

1 Thomas Gradgrind took no heed of these trivialities of course, but passed on as a practical man ought to pass on, either brushing the noisy insects from his thoughts, or consigning them to the House of Correction. But, the turning of the road took him by the back of the booth, and at the back of the booth a number of children were
5 congregated in a number of stealthy attitudes, striving to peep in at the hidden glories of the place.

This brought him to a stop. 'Now, to think of these vagabonds,' said he, 'attracting the young rabble from a model school.'

A space of stunted grass and dry rubbish being between him and the young rabble,
10 he took his eyeglass out of his waistcoat to look for any child he knew by name, and might order off. Phenomenon almost incredible though distinctly seen, what did he then behold but his own metallurgical Louisa, peeping with all her might through a hole in a deal board, and his own mathematical Thomas abasing himself on the ground to catch but a hoof of the graceful equestrian Tyrolean flower-act!

15 Dumb with amazement, Mr. Gradgrind crossed to the spot where his family was thus disgraced, laid his hand upon each erring child, and said:

'Louisa!! Thomas!!'

Both rose, red and disconcerted. But, Louisa looked at her father with more boldness than Thomas did. Indeed, Thomas did not look at him, but gave himself up to be
20 taken home like a machine.

'In the name of wonder, idleness, and folly!' said Mr. Gradgrind, leading each away by a hand; 'what do you do here?'

'Wanted to see what it was like,' returned Louisa, shortly.

'What it was like?'

25 'Yes, father.'

There was an air of jaded sullenness in them both, and particularly in the girl: yet, struggling through the dissatisfaction of her face, there was a light with nothing to rest upon, a fire with nothing to burn, a starved imagination keeping life in itself somehow, which brightened its expression. Not with the brightness natural to
30 cheerful youth, but with uncertain, eager, doubtful flashes, which had something painful in them, analogous to the changes on a blind face groping its way.

She was a child now, of fifteen or sixteen; but at no distant day would seem to become a woman all at once. Her father thought so as he looked at her. She was pretty. Would have been self-willed (he thought in his eminently practical way) but
35 for her bringing-up.

'Thomas, though I have the fact before me, I find it difficult to believe that you, with your education and resources, should have brought your sister to a scene like this.'

'I brought *him*, father,' said Louisa, quickly. 'I asked him to come.'

'I am sorry to hear it. I am very sorry indeed to hear it. It makes Thomas no better,
40 and it makes you worse, Louisa.'

She looked at her father again, but no tear fell down her cheek.

'You! Thomas and you, to whom the circle of the sciences is open; Thomas and you, who may be said to be replete with facts; Thomas and you, who have been trained to mathematical exactness; Thomas and you, here!' cried Mr. Gradgrind. 'In this
45 degraded position! I am amazed.'

'I was tired, father. I have been tired a long time,' said Louisa.

'Tired? Of what?' asked the astonished father.

'I don't know of what—of everything, I think.'

'Say not another word,' returned Mr. Gradgrind. 'You are childish. I will hear no

50 more.' He did not speak again until they had walked some half-a-mile in silence, when he gravely broke out with: 'What would your best friends say, Louisa? Do you attach no value to their good opinion? What would Mr. Bounderby say?' At the mention of this name, his daughter stole a look at him, remarkable for its intense and searching character. He saw nothing of it, for before he looked at her, she had again
55 cast down her eyes!

An extract from Charles Dickens's Hard Times

---

1. The following is a comprehension question. As such, only short answers are required.

a) What do you think a 'House of Correction' might be? [1]

b) Why do the children adopt 'stealthy attitudes'? [1]

c) Why is Gradgrind brought 'to a stop'? Is it that:

- He wants to see what the children are looking at.
- He recognises the children from the school.
- He wishes to made his disapproval known to the children.

Circle the answer that appears most correct. [1]

d) What type of animal is being featured in the show the children are trying to glimpse? [1]

e) Why do you think Gradgrind is described as 'Dumb with amazement'? [1]

2. This question tests your ability to find a quotation and explain its meaning.

a) In the opening paragraph, there is a metaphor that conveys Gradgrind's initial reaction to the circus. Please point out the metaphor, and explain how it conveys Gradgrind's opinions.

QUOTATION [1]

EXPLANATION [3]

3. This question tests your ability to discuss language. The following three quotations are taken from between lines 18 and 31. Explain how the writer conveys a sense of the children's disappointment and distress in each of them. Your ability to discuss the

meanings of individual words and to identify literary techniques (such as metaphors or similes) will be rewarded.

a) 'Both rose, red and disconcerted. But, Louisa looked at her father with more boldness than Thomas did.' [2]

b) 'Thomas did not look at him, but gave himself up to be taken home like a machine.' [3]

c) '...struggling through the dissatisfaction of her face, there was a light with nothing to rest upon, a fire with nothing to burn.' [3]

d) Look back at lines 1 – 31. What is your overall impression of Louisa? Using adjectives (describing words) and any quotation NOT used in the exam so far, write your answer below. [3 marks; 12 marks total for this question].

4. This question tests your understanding of character. Think about the character of Louisa. In your own words, explain what the following two quotations say about her character:

a) 'I brought *him*, father,' said Louisa, quickly. 'I asked him to come.' [3]

b) 'She looked at her father again, but no tear fell down her cheek.' [3]

5. This question tests your ability to explain the meanings of words as they appear in the passage. Work out the meaning of the following words based on their meaning in the passage. [6]

a) Jaded (line 26)

b) Groping (line 31)

c) Self-willed (line 34)

d) Eminently (line 34)

e) Replete (line 43)

f) Degraded (line 45)

6. This question tests your ability to explain the meanings of quotations. In your own words, and based on the context of the passage, explain why the writer has written the following:

a) '...I find it difficult to believe that you, with your education and resources, should have brought your sister to a scene like this.' [2]

b) 'I was tired, father. I have been tired a long time,' said Louisa. [3]

c) He saw nothing of it, for before he looked at her, she had again cast down her eyes! [3]

Paper Three: Model Answers & Guidance

1. The following is a comprehension question. As such, only short answers are required.

a) What do you think a 'House of Correction' might be? [1]

A prison.

A question like this really does require a specific answer. Some internal mark schemes may be kinder, and leave room for similar answers, such as: **a place where convicts are sent to be reformed; a reformatory.**

Notice how I did not use a complete sentence. This is because the question has explicitly told us that only 'short answers are required.'

b) Why do the children adopt 'stealthy attitudes'? [1]

So that they are not caught by the circus workers trying to steal a glimpse of the performance.

Answering this particular question depends on knowing what the word *stealth* means – to be stealthy is to be quiet and discreet. However, even if you know this, you then need to infer *why* the children would need to be discreet. The answer is of course that they are trying to steal a free show!

c) Why is Gradgrind brought 'to a stop'? Is it that:

i) He wants to see what the children are looking at.
ii) He recognises the children from the school.
iii) He wishes to made his disapproval known to the children.

Circle the answer that appears most correct. [1]

(iii)

You occasionally see a one-off multiple choice question in papers that are otherwise *not* multiple choice papers.

Often, one or more of the other potential answers (that is, aside from the correct one) are "semi right" – the examiners are trying to get you to distinguish between a "semi correct" answer, and a correct answer. It is true that Gradgrind does recognise the children from the school. However, while this may be the case, it seems that he is actually stopping so he can make his disapproval known. As a result, the third choice is a far more convincing answer than the second.

d) What type of animal is being featured in the show the children are trying to glimpse? [1]

A horse.

The main clue is the word equestrian, which is a word that relates to horse riding. The other clue is the mention of a hoof; though of course this is of limited use, since a hoof only winnows the list of animals down so far![1]

e) Why do you think Gradgrind is described as 'Dumb with amazement'? [1]

He has been rendered speechless, because he is so surprised to see his own children trying to glimpse the circus act.

The question here is in fact somewhat unclear. Is it asking the candidate to define

'Dumb with amazement,' or is it in fact asking why Gradgrind has been rendered 'Dumb with amazement?' Frustrating as it might be, I have seen countless unclear questions in 11+ papers from top schools – so I thought it might be wise to replicate one.

While it might be tempting to simply march out the room in protest, I personally like to see it as a reminder that the examiners are also human – because somehow that makes the whole process seem less intimidating!

My advice is – where possible – to answer the question in such a way that you cover all your bases. 'Dumb,' in this context, means unable to speak, so the expression implies that Gradgrind has been rendered speechless. He has been rendered speechless as a result of the shock of seeing his children in this circumstance. The first part of my answer gives this definition, whereas the second part gives the explanation.

2. This question tests your ability to find a quotation and explain its meaning.

a) In the opening paragraph, there is a metaphor that conveys Gradgrind's initial reaction to the circus. Please point out the metaphor, and explain how it conveys Gradgrind's opinions.

QUOTATION [1]

The metaphor is as follows: '...pass on, either brushing the noisy insects from his thoughts, or consigning them to the House of Corrections.'

EXPLANATION [3]

The metaphor, by likening the circus and its workers to 'noisy insects' that have encroached on Gradgrind's thoughts, suggests that Gradgrind sees them as a nuisance, albeit one that can be easily dismissed.[2] The invocation of the House of Corrections suggests he believes that the circus workers can and should undergo reform to bring them in line with Gradgrind's own sense of decorum.

The difficulty here is that this quote appears abruptly at the start of the passage, which may disorientate some candidates. The central part of this metaphor compares the circus workers to noisy insects; however, to get all the marks, the candidate needs to explore the fact that: a) the metaphor frames the circus workers as a nuisance; and b) that Gradgrind feels that they should be sent to be reformed.

3. This question tests your ability to discuss language. The following three quotations are taken from between lines 18 and 31. Explain how the writer conveys a sense of

the children's disappointment and distress in each of them. Your ability to discuss the meanings of individual words and to identify literary techniques (such as metaphors or similes) will be rewarded.

a) 'Both rose, red and disconcerted. But, Louisa looked at her father with more boldness than Thomas did.' [2]

> **That the children are both described as 'red' implies a state of heightened emotion, since it indicates that the children are flushed, thus hinting that they are in a state of distress – indeed, the alliteration of 'rose' and 'red' lends the image extra emphasis.[3] However, while both children are 'disconcerted' – a word that captures their being unsettled and displaying signs of distress – Louisa's 'boldness' suggests that she is willing, via her gaze, to communicate her unabashed disappointment in a way her brother is not.**

The reason the exam paper has offered up two marks for analysing this quote, yet three marks for the next two quotes, is because this quote is arguably less challenging, since it does not contain any similes or metaphors.

When the quote is made up of two short sentences (like this one is), make sure that you say something about both of the sentences, not just one of them.

I am scoring my first mark for analysing how the children are red faced and disconcerted, and for parsing that vocabulary. The second is for discussing the word 'boldness' and how it sets Louisa apart from her brother.

b) 'Thomas did not look at him, but gave himself up to be taken home like a machine.' [3]

> **The simile here, likening the way Thomas surrendered to a machine, communicates a distress so profound that it borders onto nihilism: Thomas has allowed himself to be utterly subjugated to his father's will, as if he were a mere tool at his father's disposal.[4] That Thomas 'did not look at' his father subtly telegraphs a disappointment, for it suggests a deflated and defeatist body language.**

If you are hoping to score all three marks here, it is essential that you acknowledge and analyse the simile – after all, the question itself mentions similes as one of the key language techniques you ought to be alert to.

Notice that, after analysing the simile – which I would expect to score me at least two marks – I then very quickly offer some analysis of the part of the quotation before the comma, a tactic intended to cover all my bases, and squeeze out a third mark.

c) '...struggling through the dissatisfaction of her face, there was a light with nothing to rest upon, a fire with nothing to burn.' [3]

On the most basic level, one would note the 'dissatisfaction' on Louisa's face communicates a form of disappointment: she is not satisfied. However, the pair of metaphors the writer uses gives more sophisticated insight. Her facial expression is likened to 'a light,' then 'a fire.' If her expression is a reflection of some inner qualities, there is a sense that the circumstances around her are inadequate to cater to them: they provide nothing for her inner light 'to rest upon,' and 'nothing' for her inner fire to 'burn.' As such, the writer is not only conveying Louisa's disappointment, but also her existence in an inadequate circumstance which, due to her nature, ensures her disappointment.

Again, you will only be able to secure the three marks if you can acknowledge the metaphor contained within this quote. In fact, there appears to be two metaphors: one comparing Louisa's facial expression to light, the next comparing it to 'fire.' At any rate, the candidate needs to observe this, and offer an explanation of how it conveys Louisa's despair and/or distress. Merely observing that there is a metaphor would likely limit you to just one mark.

d) Look back at lines 1 – 31. What is your overall impression of Louisa? Using adjectives (describing words) and any quotation NOT used in the exam so far, write your answer below. [3 marks; 12 marks total for this question].

An apt adjective to describe Louisa might be inquisitive; after all, when we first encounter her, she is not merely looking through the 'deal board' at the circus, but doing so 'with all her might.' The physical strain appears to convey the degree of her inquisitiveness. That we are also told she has a 'starved imagination' suggests that, while her inquisitiveness may be starved, it remains latent.[5]

Subversive is another adjective that comes to mind. Albeit subtly, Louisa pushes back against her father's authority, not simply with her transgression, but also in her standoffish justification – 'Wanted to see what it was like' – and the abruptness of her tone (she replies 'shortly,' we are told).

Finally, Louisa might be described as disorientated – not so much physically as emotionally and psychologically. This is conveyed when the narrator likens the 'flashes' that play across her face to the 'changes on a blind face groping its way.' If a blind person is disorientated physically, Louisa's face indicates that she is disorientated emotionally in her current set of circumstances.

There are resonances in this question to the question in the previous style of paper that asked us what we learned about a character within the extract. However, the difference here is that we need to be far more selective, and far more succinct – after all, this is a three mark question, so we can infer that they likely require three adjectives, each accompanied by a brief explanation.

Even though we need to be brief, it is important to try and capture the complexity of the character in question. In a sense, Louisa's inquisitiveness and defiance give her direction – and in some respects, her disorientation is in conflict to those characteristics. However, it is still there; and, by pointing it out, I indicate my sensitivity to nuance.

4. This question tests your understanding of character. Think about the character of Louisa. In your own words, explain what the following two quotations say about her character:

a) 'I brought *him*, father,' said Louisa, quickly. 'I asked him to come.' [3]

By disillusioning her father of the idea that Tom was responsible, Louisa exhibits her sense of fairness: she is not willing to let her brother take the blame for her transgression.[6] In fact, given her father's seemingly stern tone, her willingness to shoulder the blame may even be considered courageous. Furthermore, that she was the instigator shows a degree of self-possession, and perhaps a persuasive streak in her personality – after all, she not only goes on this jaunt, but also managed to enlist her brother to come along, too[7].

In a sense, this style of question is still asking you to demonstrate a close understanding of the language used. However, this time you are not required to analyse the language techniques. Instead, by making using of the 'in your own words' formula, the examiner is asking you to demonstrate understanding by offering an explanation.

There are three marks at play here, so it is important to be able to demonstrate the various lights this quote shines on Louisa's personality – her fair-mindedness, her courage, but also her relationship with her brother. Each will score you a mark apiece.

b) 'She looked at her father again, but no tear fell down her cheek.' [3]

> **Given the context of this line – it comes immediately after Gradgrind has chastised Louisa for instigating the jaunt to the circus – the absence of tears seems to indicate that she has a different worldview to her father: his condemnation does not elicit tears, because, to her mind, she has not done anything blameworthy, and thus has no reason to feel compunction.[8] That she is willing to maintain eye-contact hints at the boldness of her personality: she is not willing to physically shy away from the scolding.**

Notice how, with this quote, I've explicitly brought in its precise context within the passage in order to illuminate my answer. By using this tactic to explain how the quote suggests Louisa's worldview deviates from her father's would likely score me two marks.

Notice also how I offer an explanation of what we can infer not only from the fact Louisa does not cry, but also from the fact she intentionally seems to seek out her father's gaze. This will secure me the third mark.

5. This question tests your ability to explain the meanings of words as they appear in the passage. Work out the meaning of the following words based on their meaning in the passage. [6]

a) Jaded (line 26)

> **Jaded here means world-weary.**

b) Groping (line 21)

> **Groping here means feeling or touching.**

c) Self-willed (line 34)

> **Self-willed here suggests purposeful and obstinate.**

d) Eminently (line 34)

Eminently here means exceedingly.

e) Replete (line 43)

Replete hear means teeming.

f) Degraded (line 45)

Degraded here means debased.

6. This question tests your ability to explain the meanings of quotations. In your own words, and based on the context of the passage, explain why the writer has written the following:

a) '…I find it difficult to believe that you, with your education and resources, should have brought your sister to a scene like this.' [2]

The writer has written this primarily as a means to reiterate Gradgrind's disappointment and incredulity with his children's behaviour, and the fact that he feels as though, given his children's pedagogic regime and upbringing, they ought to have known better.[9] More subtly, it is also used to indicate Gradgrind's gender-based biases: he assumes – wrongly – that his son, not his daughter, would be the instigator.

The phrasing of this question is a bit tricky: it is not simply asking why Gradgrind says the above quote; it is asking why the writer has put those words in Gradgrind's mouth. This is an important distinction, because while Gradgrind may not be wishing to reveal his own gender-bias, for instance, the writer very clearly wishes to reveal it about him – and that is thus one of the reasons the author writes the above.

When answering a question about why the writer chose to do something, it is sensible to write in such a way that acknowledges this distinction between the writer and the character.

I score my first mark for acknowledging that the writer uses this quote to reiterate Gradgrind's disappointment in his children. I score my second for acknowledging that the writer uses it to reveal Gradgrind's sexism.

b) 'I was tired, father. I have been tired a long time,' said Louisa. [3]

The purpose of the author writing this is not only to reiterate Louisa's

weariness with her circumstances, but also to indicate that it has been a long-standing issue (indeed, the fact it has been so ongoing tacitly suggests it is more than a mere physical tiredness; it is an emotional and psychological tiredness). The author also writes this to help indicate the degree to which the lines of communication are open between father and daughter – Louisa may feel comfortable enough to verbally register her discontent, yet she is not comfortable articulating her reasons with coherent specificity.

If you merely observe that this indicates that Louisa is not just physically tired, but emotionally tired, that is worth one mark. A second depends on understanding the idea that it is a longstanding issue.

To score the third mark, a candidate needs to acknowledge that the writer includes this also as a way to reveal the larger dynamic between father and daughter.

c) He saw nothing of it, for before he looked at her, she had again cast down her eyes! [3]

The author writes this not only to demonstrate Gradgrind's obliviousness with regards to Louisa's feelings towards Bounderby, but also the fact that Louisa wishes to conceal – or perhaps feels uncomfortable disclosing – her feelings towards Bounderby. The author also writes this to create a drama that might entice the reader, since it raises the question of whether Louisa will make these feelings known to her father, and, indeed, what these feelings might be.

Observing that Gradgrind is oblivious will get you the first mark; noting that Louisa wishes to conceal her feelings will get you the second. The third is for understanding the drama and excitement this quote generates. Remember, a writer may be including something not just to be developing characters, but also to create tension and anticipation.

Paper Four: The Blithedale Romance

CLOSE LANGUAGE PAPER; DEVILISH; 40 MINUTES

This novel is set in the mid nineteenth century. The narrator, Miles Coverdale, has joined a group of idealists, who have left civilisation to live together in a small rural community. This passage takes place during their first day together – and a knock has just been heard at the front door.

1 Whether to enjoy a dramatic suspense, or that we were selfishly contrasting our own comfort with the chill and dreary situation of the unknown person at the threshold, or that some of us city folk felt a little startled at the knock which came so unseasonably, through night and storm, to the door of the lonely farmhouse—so it happened
5 that nobody, for an instant or two, arose to answer the summons. Pretty soon there came another knock. The first had been moderately loud; the second was smitten so forcibly that the knuckles of the applicant must have left their mark in the door panel.

"He knocks as if he had a right to come in," said Zenobia, laughing. "And what are we thinking of?—It must be Mr. Hollingsworth!"

10 Hereupon I went to the door, unbolted, and flung it wide open. There, sure enough, stood Hollingsworth, his shaggy greatcoat all covered with snow, so that he looked quite as much like a polar bear as a modern philanthropist.

"Sluggish hospitality this!" said he, in those deep tones of his, which seemed to come out of a chest as capacious as a barrel. "It would have served you right if I had lain
15 down and spent the night on the doorstep, just for the sake of putting you to shame. But here is a guest who will need a warmer and softer bed."

And, stepping back to the wagon in which he had journeyed hither, Hollingsworth received into his arms and deposited on the doorstep a figure enveloped in a cloak. It was evidently a woman; or, rather—judging from the ease with which he lifted her, and the little space which she seemed to fill in his arms, a slim and unsubstantial girl. As she showed some hesitation about entering the door, Hollingsworth, with his usual directness and lack of ceremony, urged her forward not merely within the entry, but into the warm and strongly lighted kitchen.

"Who is this?" whispered I, remaining behind with him, while he was taking off his greatcoat.

"Who? Really, I don't know," answered Hollingsworth, looking at me with some surprise. "It is a young person who belongs here, however; and no doubt she had been expected. Zenobia, or some of the women folks, can tell you all about it."

"I think not," said I, glancing towards the new-comer and the other occupants of the kitchen. "Nobody seems to welcome her. I should hardly judge that she was an expected guest."

"Well, well," said Hollingsworth quietly, "We'll make it right."

The stranger, or whatever she were, remained standing precisely on that spot of the kitchen floor to which Hollingsworth's kindly hand had impelled her. The cloak falling partly off, she was seen to be a very young woman dressed in a poor but decent gown, made high in the neck, and without any regard to fashion or smartness. Her brown hair fell down from beneath a hood, not in curls but with only a slight wave; her face was of a wan, almost sickly hue, betokening habitual seclusion from the sun and free atmosphere, like a flower-shrub that had done its best to blossom in too scanty light. To complete the pitiableness of her aspect, she shivered either with cold, or fear, or nervous excitement, so that you might have beheld her shadow vibrating on the fire-lighted wall. In short, there has seldom been seen so depressed and sad a figure as this young girl's; and it was hardly possible to help being angry with her, from mere despair of doing anything for her comfort. The fantasy occurred to me that she was some desolate kind of a creature, doomed to wander about in snow-storms; and that, though the ruddiness of our window panes had tempted her into a human dwelling, she would not remain long enough to melt the icicles out of her hair.

Another conjecture likewise came into my mind. Recollecting Hollingsworth's sphere of philanthropic action, I deemed it possible that he might have brought one of his guilty patients, to be wrought upon and restored to spiritual health by the pure influences which our mode of life would create.

An extract from Nathaniel Hawthorne's *The Blithedale Romance*

---

1. The following is a comprehension question. As such, only short answers are required.

a) This passage is set during what time of day? [1]

b) Why does Hollingsworth knock at the door a second time? [1]

c) Why does Zenobia laugh? Is it because:

- She finds the knocking to be ridiculous in its volume.
- She believes the knocking implies a comical sense of entitlement.
- She finds it funny to think of Hollingsworth out in the snow.

Circle the answer that appears most correct. [1]

d) Why is Hollingsworth unable to open the door himself? [1]

e) Why do you think, when Hollingsworth says "'Sluggish hospitality this!'", the writer uses an exclamation mark? [1]

2. This question tests your ability to discuss language.

The following three quotations are taken from between lines 10 and 23. Explain how the writer conveys a sense of Hollingsworth's size and gravitas in each of them. Your ability to discuss the meanings of individual words and to identify literary techniques (such as metaphors or similes) will be rewarded.

a) 'There, sure enough, stood Hollingsworth, his shaggy greatcoat all covered with snow, so that he looked quite as much like a polar bear as a modern philanthropist.' [3]

b) '...those deep tones of his, which seemed to come out of a chest as capacious as a barrel.' [3]

c) 'Hollingsworth, with his usual directness and lack of ceremony, urged her forward not merely within the entry, but into the warm and strongly lighted kitchen....' [2]

d) Look back at lines 1 – 23. What is your overall impression of Hollingsworth? Using adjectives (describing words) and any quotation NOT used in the exam so far, write your answer below. [3 marks; 12 marks total for this question].

3. This question tests your understanding of character.

Think about the character of the girl who arrives with Hollingsworth. In your own words, explain what the following two quotations say about her character:

a) 'The stranger, or whatever she were, remained standing precisely on that spot of the kitchen floor to which Hollingsworth's kindly hand had impelled her...' [3]

b) '...it was hardly possible to help being angry with her, from mere despair of doing anything for her comfort.' [3]

4. This question tests your ability to explain the meanings of words as they appear in the passage. Work out the meaning of the following words based on their meaning in the passage. [6]

a) Unsubstantial (line 20)

b) Smartness (line 36)

c) Habitual (line 38)

d) Pitiableness (line 40)

e) Desolate (line 45)

f) Dwelling (line 47)

5. This question tests your ability to find a quotation and explain its meaning.

Hollingsworth's professional work prior to joining this community is referenced in this passage. Please point out a quote that identifies his profession, and explain what you think his work entailed.

QUOTATION [1]

EXPLANATION [3]

6. This question tests your ability to explain the meanings of quotations.

In your own words, and based on the context of the passage, explain why the writer has written the following:

a) '"Who? Really, I don't know," answered Hollingsworth, looking at me with some surprise.' [3]

b) 'Nobody seems to welcome her. I should hardly judge that she was an expected guest.' [3]

c) 'The fantasy occurred to me that she was some desolate kind of a creature, doomed to wander about in snow-storms.' [2]

Paper Four: Model Answers & Guidance

1. The following is a comprehension question. As such, only short answers are required.

a) This passage is set during what time of day? [1]

Night-time

To score the mark, you need to be able to spot this detail, which appears in line x: 'through night and storm.' The word 'night' would also get the mark.

Again, notice how the question is explicitly telling us that 'only short answers are required.' This is a cue to indicate we can dispense with full sentences for this question.

b) Why does Hollingsworth knock at the door a second time? [1]

He does so because nobody responded to him when he knocked the first time.

Any answer than acknowledges that he was forced to do so because his first knock was ignored will score the mark.

c) Why does Zenobia laugh? Is it because:

i) She finds the knocking to be ridiculous in its volume.

ii) She believes the knocking implies a comical sense of entitlement.

iii) She finds it funny to think of Hollingsworth out in the snow.

Circle the answer that appears most correct. [1]

(ii)

The first option (i) is the one that is trying to mislead you, since it does seem to be true that Zenobia finds the volume of the knocking to be ridiculous. However, it is Hollingsworth's sense of entitlement that actually elicits her laughter, which means that the second option (ii) is 'most correct.'

d) Why is Hollingsworth unable to open the door himself?

He is unable to do so because it is bolted.

This question requires a keen eye. When Coverdale goes to open the door, the word 'unbolted' is used – and this is the clue they are expecting you to spot.

e) Why do you think, when Hollingsworth says '"Sluggish hospitality this!"', the writer uses an exclamation mark? [1]

It lends the comment emphasis, communicating the degree of his frustration towards the slow response.

Any response that acknowledges that it adds emphasis to his frustration will score the mark.

2. This question tests your ability to discuss language.

The following three quotations are taken from between lines 10 and 23. Explain how the writer conveys a sense of Hollingsworth's size and gravitas in each of them. Your ability to discuss the meanings of individual words and to identify literary techniques (such as metaphors or similes) will be rewarded.

a) 'There, sure enough, stood Hollingsworth, his shaggy greatcoat all covered with snow, so that he looked quite as much like a polar bear as a modern philanthropist.' [3]

The central simile of this sentence, which likens Hollingsworth's physical appearance to that of a polar bear, is not only a means to draw attention to the fact his coat is covered in snow; it also more subtly invites the reader to envisage his epic proportions, and to associate Hollingsworth with the regality and dignity polar bears evoke. Moreover, the pacing of the sentence, in which an interpolated phrase ('sure enough') slows the rhythm and creates suspense, affords the phrase 'stood Hollingsworth' additional ceremony.

Correctly identifying the simile the author uses is almost certainly good to win you a mark; and the two extra observations I've included – that it emphasises the degree to which he is covered in snow, and his colossal dimensions – are likely to be worth an extra mark apiece. However, to play it safe and ensure no marks slip through the net, I have also pointed out how language is used to impact the pacing, and, as a result, further emphasise Hollingsworth's gravitas.

b) '...those deep tones of his, which seemed to come out of a chest as capacious as a barrel.' [3]

The simile in this quote, which likens the dimensions of Hollingsworth's chest to those of a barrel, not only emphasises his physical stature, but also underscores the gravitas to his voice: it is suggesting that his 'deep tones' have a reverberating, booming quality to them. However, the use of the word 'seemed' is interesting, since it implies that there is some ambiguity to the provenance of the sound, tacitly suggesting that it has a transcendent, otherworldly quality that evokes gravitas.[1]

Again, identifying the simile will score you the first mark, and pointing out that it emphasises his size and the booming quality of his voice, will almost certainly be enough to score you the second and third mark.

However, true to form, I have also added a quick bit of analysis about the word 'seemed,' and how the ambiguity it creates further add to the gravitas. Again, this is from an abundance of caution – I do not want to give them any excuse not to award me all three marks.

c) 'Hollingsworth, with his usual directness and lack of ceremony, urged her forward not merely within the entry, but into the warm and strongly lighted kitchen....' [2]

That Hollingsworth's 'directness and lack of ceremony' is described as 'usual' subtly evokes gravitas, since it suggests he is the subject of others' observations, and that his habits are worthy of remembering. The forcefulness with which he 'urges' the girl 'forward' – she is pushed not 'merely' into the entry, but right inside the 'kitchen' – telegraphs his dimensions: he is not only moving another person as if they were a chess piece, but he is also moving them a considerable distance.

This particular quote has two marks up for grabs, and this is because there are no similes or metaphors in play. The way in which he moves the girl forward such a great distance, and how this reflects on his own size, is worth a mark. A second mark could be gained for remarking on how the word 'usual' indicates that he is someone others take note of.

If you instead looked at how the 'lack of ceremony' also indicates gravitas – because it suggests that Hollingsworth already has enough innate gravitas – that would also be worthy of a mark. Also, analysing the word 'directness' in more depth, and discussing how his shoot-from-the-hip manner enhances his air of gravitas, would also score you a mark.

d) Look back at lines 1 – 23. What is your overall impression of Hollingsworth? Using adjectives (describing words) and any quotation NOT used in the exam so far, write your answer below. [3 marks; 12 marks total for this question].

Hollingsworth might be described as unabashed, given that he proceeds without shame or apology. For instance, although he knocks on the door with absurd gusto – 'so forcibly' that the narrator believes Hollingsworth surely left a 'mark in the door-panel' – Hollingsworth is utterly unapologetic for this excessive approach.[2]

Hollingsworth also appears to have a distinct self-righteous streak to him.[3] **This is perhaps best exemplified when he dresses down the inhabitants of the farm for their keeping him out in the cold, asserting that he ought to have slept outside if only 'for the sake of putting them to shame.' That he wishes to induce shame in them hints at his sense of moral superiority – implicit is Hollingsworth's belief that he would never have committed such a supposed sin.**

Despite Hollingsworth's sanctimoniousness, another adjective to

describe him might be kind, since he is undoubtedly exhibiting this quality when dealing with the 'unsubstantial girl.'[4] This is conveyed in his desire to ensure she has a 'warmer and softer bed' in which to sleep, but also in the sheer fact he has brought her with him and included her in the group.

The mark scheme for this will not contain an exhaustive list of adjectives you can use. Instead, the examiner will be looking for any three adjectives that work, combined with a mature explanation of the reasoning behind your choice.

3. This question tests your understanding of character.

Think about the character of the girl who arrives with Hollingsworth. In your own words, explain what the following two quotations say about her character:

a) 'The stranger, or whatever she were, remained standing precisely on that spot of the kitchen floor to which Hollingsworth's kindly hand had impelled her...' [3]

That the young girl seems unwilling to move from where she stands seems to suggest a reticence and diffidence: she feels that moving would elicit unwanted attention, and might be construed as an attempt to engage in social intercourse. Moreover, Coverdale's uncertainty that she can even be described as a stranger suggests that the girl exudes a sense of mystery that defies categorisation.

The examiner is looking for the candidate to acknowledge that the fact the girl is rooted to the spot communicates that she shy/reticent – this would win the first mark. The second mark would be available for making a sensible comment about the mystery evoked from Coverdale's aside, in which he hints that he is not sure he can even safely call her a stranger.

The third mark for this particular question is likely set aside for the overall flair and sophistication of your answer.

b) '...it was hardly possible to help being angry with her, from mere despair of doing anything for her comfort.' [3]

This quotation suggests that the girl is a figure of such extreme pathos that the sympathy she elicits in Coverdale is so uncomfortable as to be infuriating.[5] However, though the extremes of sympathy the girl induces

may kindle anger, it is nevertheless a galvanising force, since Coverdale does express a desire to help her – she is a powerfully pitiable character.[6]

The two content marks here are for acknowledging: a) the pathos the girl induces is infuriating; and b) that the pathos she induces inspires others to take action. Again, the third mark is for expressing these points with flair.

4. This question tests your ability to explain the meanings of words as they appear in the passage. Work out the meaning of the following words based on their meaning in the passage. (6)

a) Unsubstantial (line 20)

Unsubstantial here means diminutive.

b) Smartness (line 36)

Smartness here means tidiness.

c) Habitual (line 38)

Habitual here means sustained.

d) Pitiableness (line 40)

Pitiableness here means patheticness.

e) Desolate (line 45)

Desolate here means forsaken.

f) Dwelling (line 47)

Dwelling here means home or abode.

5. This question tests your ability to find a quotation and explain its meaning.

Hollingsworth's professional work prior to joining this community is referenced in this passage. Please point out a quote that identifies his profession, and explain what you think his work entailed.

QUOTATION [1]

'Recollecting Hollingsworth's sphere of philanthropic action...'

There are in fact two quotes in the passage that would win you this mark. The other quote is: "he looked quite as much like a polar bear as a modern philanthropist."

EXPLANATION [3]

A philanthropist is someone who works to help others through charitable action; so, on the most basic level, this is apparently what Hollingsworth had engaged in. Moreover, when Coverdale posits that perhaps the girl is one of Hollingsworth's 'guilty patients' who he might have brought along in hopes of restoring her 'spiritual health,' it suggests that he has perhaps worked with offenders, or even criminals, and helped reform and rehabilitate them.

The first mark is for offering a definition of a philanthropist. The next two marks are for inferring what sort of philanthropy Hollingsworth has previously engaged in.

The tricky thing about this question for some candidates will be defining the word philanthropist. However, if you didn't know the word, you would still arguably have been able to deduce from the passage's final paragraph that it was someone who helps others, or someone who helps others to reform their way of life. Even though the latter is a somewhat narrow definition of "philanthropist", the examiner – if a candidate has written this narrower definition – may well be willing to hand over the mark, since they can see that the candidate has made a sensible effort to deduce the definition.

6. This question tests your ability to explain the meanings of quotations.

In your own words, and based on the context of the passage, explain why the writer has written the following:

a) '"Who? Really, I don't know," answered Hollingsworth, looking at me with some surprise.' [3]

The author has written this on the most basic level to communicate that Hollingsworth does not know (or at least is claiming not to know) the girl's identity. However, the author has also written this to offer insight, ambiguous though it may be, into the dynamic between Coverdale and Hollingsworth. Hollingsworth's seeming surprise at the question might

be a result of not expecting to be queried, but may equally signify surprise at Coverdale's continued presence. Equally, while Hollingsworth's repeating of the word 'Who?' may be intended purely to clarify, the writer may also be using its abruptness as a means to again convey Hollingsworth's shock at encountering Coverdale.

Again, we have been asked to write in our own words for these questions, so please ensure that you do so.

The first mark is for recognising that the author includes this quote in order to make clear Hollingsworth's official line on the young girl – that he does not know who she is. The other two marks can be won for discussing how this quote offers insight into Coverdale and Hollingsworth's relationship, though you'll need to have some sophistication to your response to score both marks.

b) 'Nobody seems to welcome her. I should hardly judge that she was an expected guest.' [3]

The author writes this to convey the girl's social isolation – after all, it makes clear that nobody is engaging with her – and to raise the possibility that she is in fact gate crashing this community.[7] The writer includes this also to present Coverdale as an observant individual, attuned to social dynamics, and to demonstrate his desire to treat Hollingsworth as a confidante. Finally, the writer uses this to cast Coverdale as a voyeur: he remarks on others' inaction, yet ironically does not take action himself.[8]

By acknowledging how this quote is used to emphasise the girl's social isolation, you will be in a position to score the first mark here. To score the other two, you need to make some sophisticated observations regarding how this quote shines light on Coverdale and his relationship to Hollingsworth.

c) 'The fantasy occurred to me that she was some desolate kind of a creature, doomed to wander about in snow-storms.' [2]

The author has written this to heighten the sense of mystery and allure surrounding the girl: the notion of her being entrapped by fate, and that she might somehow be a nomad of perpetual blizzards, grants her a quasi-mystical status.[9] Moreover, the author writes this to further convey

Coverdale's personality: he is an individual with a rich imaginative life, who is prone to daydreaming.

You'll get a mark for acknowledging that the quote lends the girl an air of mystery, and the second for pointing out how it draws attention to Coverdale's tendency to daydream.

Line By Line Papers

Note: This style of paper has more in common with the Close Language Paper than it does the All Rounder Paper, because, like the Close Language Paper, much of the paper is comprised of low-scoring, quick-fire questions. That said, there is a 'mini essay' style question right at the end of this paper, which is reminiscent of the longer questions in the All Rounder Paper.

As you'll be able to see – and as the name suggests – the paper goes through the extract in a linear fashion. The most popular types of questions in this paper are those that require us to sleuth out answers, and those that ask us to explain things in our own words.

Both of the Line By Line papers I've included here are out of a total of thirty-five marks.

Paper Five: The Man Who Was Thursday

LINE BY LINE PAPER; DIFFICULT; 40 MINUTES

This is an extract from a novel set in the 1900s. Syme is an undercover police officer who has infiltrated an anarchist terrorist group, but is fearful that the group are suspicious of him. In this passage, Syme, after eating lunch, spots one of the terrorists: Professor de Worms.

---

1 He had taken his seat in the upper room of the restaurant, which was full of the chink of knives and the chatter of foreigners. He remembered that in old days he had imagined that all these harmless and kindly aliens were anarchists. He shuddered, remembering the real thing. But even the shudder had the delightful shame of
5 escape. The wine, the common food, the familiar place, the faces of natural and talkative men, made him almost feel as if the Council of the Seven Days had been a bad dream; and although he knew it was nevertheless an objective reality, it was at least a distant one. Tall houses and populous streets lay between him and his last sight of the shameful seven; he was free in free London, and drinking wine among the free. With
10 a somewhat easier action, he took his hat and stick and strolled down the stair into the shop below.

When he entered that lower room he stood stricken and rooted to the spot. At a small table, close up to the blank window and the white street of snow, sat the old anarchist Professor over a glass of milk, with his lifted livid face and pendent eyelids. For an
15 instant Syme stood as rigid as the stick he leant upon. Then with a gesture as of blind hurry, he brushed past the Professor, dashing open the door and slamming it behind him, and stood outside in the snow.

"Can that old corpse be following me?" he asked himself, biting his yellow moustache. "I stopped too long up in that room, so that even such leaden feet could catch me up. One comfort is, with a little brisk walking I can put a man like that as far away as Timbuctoo. Or am I too fanciful? Was he really following me? Surely Sunday would not be such a fool as to send a lame man?"

He set off at a smart pace, twisting and whirling his stick, in the direction of Covent Garden. As he crossed the great market the snow increased, growing blinding and bewildering as the afternoon began to darken. The snow-flakes tormented him like a swarm of silver bees. Getting into his eyes and beard, they added their unremitting futility to his already irritated nerves; and by the time that he had come at a swinging pace to the beginning of Fleet Street, he lost patience, and finding a Sunday teashop, turned into it to take shelter. He ordered another cup of black coffee as an excuse. Scarcely had he done so, when Professor de Worms hobbled heavily into the shop, sat down with difficulty and ordered a glass of milk.

Syme's walking-stick had fallen from his hand with a great clang, which confessed the concealed steel. But the Professor did not look round. Syme, who was commonly a cool character, was literally gaping as a rustic gapes at a conjuring trick. He had seen no cab following; he had heard no wheels outside the shop; to all mortal appearances the man had come on foot. But the old man could only walk like a snail, and Syme had walked like the wind. He started up and snatched his stick, half crazy with the contradiction in mere arithmetic, and swung out of the swinging doors, leaving his coffee untasted. An omnibus going to the Bank went rattling by with an unusual rapidity. He had a violent run of a hundred yards to reach it; but he managed to spring, swaying upon the splash-board and, pausing for an instant to pant, he climbed on to the top. When he had been seated for about half a minute, he heard behind him a sort of heavy and asthmatic breathing.

Turning sharply, he saw rising gradually higher and higher up the omnibus steps a top hat soiled and dripping with snow, and under the shadow of its brim the short-sighted face and shaky shoulders of Professor de Worms. He let himself into a seat with characteristic care, and wrapped himself up to the chin in the mackintosh rug.

Every movement of the old man's tottering figure and vague hands, every uncertain gesture and panic-stricken pause, seemed to put it beyond question that he was helpless, that he was in the last imbecility of the body. He moved by inches, he let himself down with little gasps of caution. And yet, unless the philosophical entities called time and space have no vestige even of a practical existence, it appeared quite unquestionable that he had run after the omnibus.

An extract from G. K. Chesterton's The Man Who Was Thursday

1. Lines 1-11

What is the name of the terrorist organisation Syme has infiltrated? [1]

2. Between lines 1-11, what is it about the restaurant that seemed different to Syme? [2]

3. Explain what is meant by the following sentence: 'But even the shudder had the delightful shame of escape.' [2]

4. Lines 5-11

Identify three things that cause Syme to feel more relaxed while eating lunch. [3]

5. Lines 18-22

What two reasons does Syme give for feeling unconcerned about Professor de Worms's presence in the restaurant? [2]

6. Lines 23-29

In your own words, explain why Syme entered the tearoom. [2]

7. Lines 25-34

In your own words, explain the meaning of the following:

a) Getting into his eyes and beard, they added their unremitting futility to his already irritated nerves. [2]

b) Syme, who was commonly a cool character, was literally gaping as a rustic gapes at a conjuring trick. [2]

8. Lines 25-37

In your own words, explain why Syme was surprised to see Professor de Worms arrive shortly after him at the teashop. [2]

9. Lines 37-38

At lines 37 to 38 it says 'He started up and snatched his stick, half crazy with the contradiction in mere arithmetic.' Explain what you think this could mean. [3]

10. Lines 39-42

How do we know that Syme exerted himself to get on the omnibus? Looking at lines 39-42, find two phrases that tell you this. [4]

11. Lines 51-53

At lines 51 to 53, it says: 'unless the philosophical entities called time and space have no vestige even of a practical existence, it appeared quite unquestionable that he had run after the omnibus.' What does this mean? [2]

12. Using the whole passage, explain how the writer uses language to make Syme's attempt to escape from Professor de Worms exciting. Use short quotations to support your answer. [8]

Paper Five: Model Answers & Guidance

1. Lines 1-11

What is the name of the terrorist organisation Syme has infiltrated? [1]

The organisation's name is the Council of the Seven Days.

You need to have the exact answer I've given above to secure this mark. It is simply a case of reading the passage carefully. However, you'll notice that the examiner has prefaced the question with an indication of where within the passage the answer will be located. Be sure to pay close attention to clues of this kind.

Notice also that my answer is a full sentence – as mentioned elsewhere, we should only dispense with full sentences when given explicit permission to do so.

2. Between lines 1-11, what is it about the restaurant that seemed different to Syme? [2]

Whereas he had previously imagined that the foreigners who frequent the restaurant had been anarchists, the clientele – though still almost exclusively foreign people – now seem benign to Syme.

You will only score one mark if you just mention how the foreign clientele at the restaurant now seem benign. To score both marks, you need to mention how Syme had previously perceived these foreign clientele as suspicious.

3. Explain what is meant by the following sentence: 'But even the shudder had the delightful shame of escape.' [2]

> **Syme takes a pleasure reflecting on the fearsome nature of the anarchists he had encountered, because he is currently beyond their grasp. However, the pleasure he feels is also somewhat shameful – hence the oxymoron 'delightful shame' – since he feels as if there is cowardice in having extricated himself from their company.**[1]

The first mark is for understanding that Syme takes pleasure from having escaped the company of the anarchists. However, to score the second mark, you *must* be able to pick up on the paradoxical/oxymoronic nature of this pleasure.[2]

4. Lines 5-11

Identify three things that cause Syme to feel more relaxed while eating lunch. [3]

> a) **The food and drink he was consuming.**
>
> b) **The familiarity of the restaurant in which he was dining.**
>
> c) **The sight of other men as they conversed with one another.**

It is possible that, if you had invoked Syme's awareness of the 'tall houses and populous streets' separating him from the anarchists as one of your answers, a generous examiner might be inclined to give you a mark.

However, you would not be given two separate marks if you had said the food and the drink as two separate points. After all, there are clearly other strong answers candidates had available instead.

5. Lines 18-22

What two reasons does Syme give for feeling unconcerned about Professor de Worms's presence in the restaurant? [2]

> a) **He does not believe that Sunday – presumably the anarchists'**

ringleader – would be so foolhardy as to dispatch the infirm de Worms to keep tabs on him.

b) **He feels confident that, because he can easily outpace de Worms, there will be little difficulty escaping his potential attempt to surveil him.**

Again, if the paper is prefacing the question with an indication of the lines between which you ought to look, take careful note: the answers will invariably be lurking within that bracket.

The examiners will be looking for the two answers I have given above. You probably do not have to explicitly spell out that Sunday seems to be the anarchists' ringleader, as long as your answer makes it implicitly clear that you understand this is likely the case.

6. Lines 23-29

In your own words, explain why Syme entered the tearoom. [2]

Syme entered the tearoom chiefly because of the snow, which had become increasingly heavy, and was causing him not inconsiderable physical discomfort – so much so that he eventually got to the end of his tether and sought shelter in the tearoom.

You would likely get a single mark for simply acknowledging the fact that the snow drives him inside. The extra mark is reserved for explaining how the snow makes the outdoors uncomfortable.

7. Lines 25-34

In your own words, explain the meaning of the following:

a) Getting into his eyes and beard, they added their unremitting futility to his already irritated nerves. [2]

The arbitrary and relentless nature of the snow induces in the already annoyed Syme a particular brand of irritation. Its lack of purpose and intentionality as it pelts him – it persists simply due to coincidence of natural circumstances, and is destined to merely evaporate and fall time and again – is almost more psychologically exasperating than if it had a reason to pelt him.

If you only acknowledge that Syme is already annoyed, and that the snow is making him more so, you will find yourself capped at one mark. To get the second mark, you need to be able to explain what the author is trying to convey with the (tricky) expression 'unremitting futility.'

b) Syme, who was commonly a cool character, was literally gaping as a rustic gapes at a conjuring trick. [2]

> **Whereas Syme is generally an unflustered individual, on this occasion, he has the wide-open mouth of an individual encountering something they find both extremely surprising and beyond their comprehension. The simile, by likening the cause of his surprise to a magician's illusion, also hints that de Worms's feat might in fact be the result of a deception.**

The first mark is for understanding that this sentence is conveying the fact that Syme is usually calm, but this time is very much not so. To get the second mark, you need to explain how the simile adds to our understanding.

8. Lines 25-37

In your own words, explain why Syme was surprised to see Professor de Worms arrive shortly after him at the teashop. [2]

> **Aside from the fact that Syme was not entirely convinced that Professor de Worms is tailing him in the first place, Worms is also, to all appearances, in a state of extreme infirmity. Given that Syme walked over to the teashop with considerable pace, and had covered a fair distance since leaving the restaurant, he does not reasonably expect the infirm de Worms to have been able to have made the journey almost as quickly as he had been able to do.**

One mark is for acknowledging that de Worms appears to be in a state of extreme infirmity; the second is for understanding how Syme's quick pace in walking to the tearoom ought to have been impossible for de Worms to replicate.

Notice that I have included another quick reason – namely, that Syme was initially not entirely convinced de Worms was following him. Including this is another instance of my playing it safe mentality.

9. Lines 37-38

At lines 37-38 it says 'He started up and snatched his stick, half crazy with the contradiction in mere arithmetic.' Explain what you think this could mean. [3]

> **The phrase 'contradiction in arithmetic' points to the fact that the situation does not seem to add up: de Worms cannot both be in a state of extreme infirmity, yet also able to keep up with Syme's swift walk through the city. The seeming paradox of this not only induces a desire in Syme to flee the situation, but also seems to be impacting on his psychological stability.**

If you only point out that the quote indicates that, to Syme, the situation does not seem to make sense, you will likely only get one mark. To secure the other two, you need to explain: a) how the phrase 'contradiction in arithmetic' offers insight into why the situation does not make sense to Syme; and b) the psychological impact implied by the phrase 'half crazy.'

10. Lines 39-42

How do we know that Syme exerted himself to get on the omnibus? Looking at lines 39-42, find two phrases that tell you this. [4]

a) **'He had a violent run of a hundred yards to reach it.'**

b) **'Pausing for an instant to pant.'**

These are the best two phrases. If you did the following quote – 'to spring, swaying upon the splash-board' – it would likely earn you one mark (as opposed to two), as although 'spring' is a kinetic verb, it is slightly less explicit that it is an exertion.[3]

11. Lines 51-53

At lines 51-53, it says: 'unless the philosophical entities called time and space have no vestige even of a practical existence, it appeared quite unquestionable that he had run after the omnibus.' What does this mean? [2]

> **This particular quote is observing how, given the constraints of Newtonian physics, it is not possible for de Worms to have boarded the omnibus without having moved at a pace equivalent to a run.[4] This therefore suggests that one of two things must be true: either de Worms**

did indeed run for the bus, or the physical laws governing the universe have been suspended.

To get both marks – as opposed to just one – you need to do slightly more than acknowledge that this quote suggests that the only logical explanation is that de Worms ran for the bus. You need to also explain *how* this is presented as the only logical explanation.

12. Using the whole passage, explain how the writer uses language to make Syme's attempt to escape from Professor de Worms exciting. Use short quotations to support your answer. [8]

A key mechanism the writer uses to create excitement is the portrayal of Syme's excited emotional state, which acts as an invitation for the reader to vicariously experience these emotions in parallel. From the instant he sets eyes on de Worms, Syme's excitement and agitation are clear: the narrator first talks about him being 'as rigid as the stick he leant on' – the simile conveying how the shock led to momentary paralysis – then notes how Syme exits with 'a gesture of blind hurry,' the word 'blind' pointing to an agitation so extreme that it momentarily suspends his vision. The sense of Syme's emotional excitement persists through the passage: the way his 'walking-stick' falls 'from his hand,' for instance, tacitly communicates a spike in agitation. By vividly conveying Syme's excitement, the writer ensures to reader feels excited, too

The writer also generates excitement through his Gothic portrayal of de Worms. The initial description of him as having 'pendent eyelids' lends him a cadaverous quality, and the writer doubles down with this motif, alliteratively describing him as 'hobbl[ing] heavily' as he enters the tearoom, and drawing attention to his 'heavy and asthmatic breathing' and his 'tottering figure' as he appears on the omnibus.[5] That he is depicted as excessively weak – 'he was in the last imbecility of his body' – paradoxically renders his relentlessness all the more disconcerting and inexplicable. Moreover, the writer adds another layer of horror with de Worms's milk drinking: he is spotted 'over a glass of milk,' and orders 'a glass of milk' in the tearoom. Given that milk drinking is usually associated with infants and their mother's milk, there is something unnervingly taboo about de Worms's penchant for it.[6] Therefore, insofar as horror induces excitement, the writer's Gothic depiction of de Worms invariably adds to the sequence's excitement.

Excitement is also conjured through the writer's atmospheric depiction of the weather. As Syme heads 'in the direction of Covent Garden,' the reader is told how 'the snow increased, growing blinding and bewildering' – the alliteration on 'blinding' and 'bewildering' adding emphasis to words that cast the weather as menacing: something that neuters the senses and disorientates. A Gothic quality is also projected onto the weather with the motif of premature nightfall: 'the afternoon began to darken.' If there was any ambiguity that the weather ought to be construed as menacing, the writer then uses a simile likening the snowflakes to 'a swarm of silver bees.' Again, the menacing and atmospheric depiction of the weather adds another layer of excitement to the passage.

After a litany of quick-fire questions, this paper ends with a 'mini essay' type question, reminiscent of the ones we saw in the All Rounder Paper.

A key difference to the mini essays we saw in the All Rounder Paper is that this question is asking us to focus explicitly on '*how the writer uses language*.' So whereas in the All Rounder Paper we had room to discuss things like free indirect style, this time we want to be laser-focused on just the language.

Of course, eight marks does not mean you need eight separate points. On the contrary, my tactic above has been to make three strong points, and to write each with enough detail to ensure that each paragraph is worth three marks (yes, I know the marks for this question is capped at eight – but my mentality is to ensure that I am giving the examiner no excuse not to award me full marks).

As ever, I put together a little plan before I started writing.

- Vivid description of Syme's agitation.
- Gothic portrayal of de Worms as cadaverous and relentless.
- Portrayal of the setting, which in turn creates atmosphere.

As I have mentioned in the foreword, there are often alternative points that a candidate might discuss that would also be worthy of scoring marks. To illustrate, I'll add another paragraph below that would also answer the question, and which I would imagine might be worth two or three marks.

Excitement is also created through the contrast between the calm of the passage's opening, and the thrills that follow – the initial calm acting to heighten the drama that ensues. That Syme is 'free in free London' lulls

the reader into a false sense of security – the repetition of 'free' almost hypnotically calming – and so too does the fact he is 'drinking wine,' an activity associated with relaxation and calm. By using language to create an air of calm at the start of the passage, the writer ensures that the action that follows is all the more shocking.

Paper Six: Wuthering Heights

LINE BY LINE PAPER; DEVILISH; 40 MINUTES

In this passage, the narrator – Mr Lockwood – is spending the night at Wuthering Heights, a mansion owned by his landlord, Mr Heathcliff. This passage starts with Mr Lockwood waking up in the middle of the night.

---

1 This time, I remembered I was lying in the oak closet, and I heard distinctly the gusty wind, and the driving of the snow; I heard, also, the fir bough repeat its teasing sound, and ascribed it to the right cause: but it annoyed me so much, that I resolved to silence it, if possible; and, I thought, I rose and endeavoured to unhasp the
5 casement.

The hook was soldered into the staple: a circumstance observed by me when awake, but forgotten.

'I must stop it, nevertheless!' I muttered, knocking my knuckles through the glass, and stretching an arm out to seize the importunate branch; instead of which, my fingers
10 closed on the fingers of a little, ice-cold hand!

The intense horror of nightmare came over me: I tried to draw back my arm, but the hand clung to it, and a most melancholy voice sobbed,

'Let me in—let me in!'

'Who are you?' I asked, struggling, meanwhile, to disengage myself.

'Catherine Linton,' it replied, shiveringly (why did I think of *Linton*? I had read *Earnshaw* twenty times for Linton)—'I'm come home: I'd lost my way on the moor!'

As it spoke, I discerned, obscurely, a child's face looking through the window. Terror made me cruel; and, finding it useless to attempt shaking the creature off, I pulled its wrist on to the broken pane, and rubbed it to and fro till the blood ran down and soaked the bedclothes: still it wailed, 'Let me in!' and maintained its tenacious grip, almost maddening me with fear.

'How can I!' I said at length. 'Let *me* go, if you want me to let you in!'

The fingers relaxed, I snatched mine through the hole, hurriedly piled the books up in a pyramid against it, and stopped my ears to exclude the lamentable prayer.

I seemed to keep them closed above a quarter of an hour; yet, the instant I listened again, there was the doleful cry moaning on!

'Begone!' I shouted. 'I'll never let you in, not if you beg for twenty years.'

'It is twenty years,' mourned the voice: 'twenty years. I've been a waif for twenty years!'

Thereat began a feeble scratching outside, and the pile of books moved as if thrust forward.

I tried to jump up; but could not stir a limb; and so yelled aloud, in a frenzy of fright.

To my confusion, I discovered the yell was not ideal: hasty footsteps approached my chamber door; somebody pushed it open, with a vigorous hand, and a light glimmered through the squares at the top of the bed. I sat shuddering yet, and wiping the perspiration from my forehead: the intruder appeared to hesitate, and muttered to himself.

At last, he said, in a half-whisper, plainly not expecting an answer, 'Is any one here?'

I considered it best to confess my presence; for I knew Heathcliff's accents, and feared he might search further, if I kept quiet. With this intention, I turned and opened the panels. I shall not soon forget the effect my action produced.

Heathcliff stood near the entrance, in his shirt and trousers; with a candle dripping over his fingers, and his face as white as the wall behind him. The first creak of the oak startled him like an electric shock: the light leaped from his hold to a distance of some feet, and his agitation was so extreme, that he could hardly pick it up.

'It is only your guest, sir,' I called out, desirous to spare him the humiliation of exposing his cowardice further. 'I had the misfortune to scream in my sleep, owing to a frightful nightmare. I'm sorry I disturbed you.'

An extract from Emily Brontë's *Wuthering Heights*

---

1. Lines 1-5

What three things does Lockwood believe he can hear upon waking up. [3]

2. Lines 6-11

In order to deal with the scratching against the outside of the window, why was Lockwood forced to thrust his knuckle through the glass? [1]

3. Explain what is meant by the following: 'The intense horror of nightmare came over me.' [2]

4. Lines 15-21

In your own words, explain why Lockwood rubs the girl's wrist against the broken glass. [2]

5. In your own words, explain the meaning of the following:

a) Why did I think of *Linton*? I had read *Earnshaw* twenty times for Linton' [2]

b) '...maintained its tenacious grip, almost maddening me with fear.' [2]

6. Lines 23-24

Once Lockwood has escaped the girl's grip, what two things does Lockwood do in an attempt to insulate himself from the girl? [2]

7. Lines 28-29

At lines 28 to 29 it says the following: "It is twenty years,' mourned the voice: 'twenty years. I've been a waif for twenty years!' Explain what you think this could mean. [3]

8. Lines 28-32

In your own words, explain why Lockwood yells at line 32. [2]

9. Lines 39-41

Between lines 39-41, what reason does Lockwood give for making his presence known to Heathcliff? [2]

10. Lines 42-45

How do we know that Heathcliff is in a state of high anxiety after Lockwood opens the panels? Looking at lines 42-45, find two phrases that tell you this.[4]

11. Lines 46-47

At lines 46-47, Lockwood asserts that he was: 'desirous to spare him the humiliation of exposing his cowardice further.' What does this mean? [2]

12. Using the whole passage, explain how the writer uses language to make this sequence terrifying. Use short quotations to support your answer. [8]

Paper Six: Model Answers & Guidance

1. Lines 1-5

What three things does Lockwood believe he can hear upon waking up. [3]

a) **The gusting of the wind.**

b) **The heavy snowfall.**

c) **The branch of a tree against the window.**

Unless they are asking for a quote, I would write an answer to a question like this in your own words – though, unlike an 'in your own words' question, you don't need to be too worried if you do end up using some of the same words that appear in the passage.

2. Lines 6-11

In order to deal with the scratching against the outside of the window, why was Lockwood forced to thrust his knuckle through the glass? [1]

Lockwood was forced to break through the glass because the window was soldered in place.

I have used a full sentence here, because we have not been given permission to do otherwise.

You would also gain the mark if you said the window was locked or sealed.

3. Explain what is meant by the following: 'The intense horror of nightmare came over me.' [2]

> **This sentence suggests that Lockwood was seized by a sense of extreme terror, though there is ambiguity whether he is suggesting that the terror was akin to that induced by a nightmare, or whether he believed this was actually a literal nightmare. It seems, in fact, that the ambiguity is intentional: Lockwood is unsure which one is true.**

You will get a mark for acknowledging that the sentence suggests Lockwood was experiencing a nightmarish terror. However, to score both marks, you need to acknowledge that it also hints that it may actually be a literal nightmare.

4. Lines 15-21

In your own words, explain why Lockwood rubs the girl's wrist against the broken glass. [2]

> **On the most basic level, Lockwood rubs the girl's wrist against the glass because his attempts to struggle free of her grip had proven unsuccessful. However, it also appears that the particularly violent nature of this gambit was borne out of fear, which was induced, it seems, by a combination of factors: the girl's ghostly, freezing-cold grip, the haunting timbre of her voice, and the unnervingly youthful face Lockwood glimpses.**

The first mark is for acknowledging that he has been unable to get free using other methods. The second is for acknowledging that his action is motivated also by fear.

5. In your own words, explain the meaning of the following:

a) Why did I think of *Linton*? I had read *Earnshaw* twenty times for Linton' [2]

> **The fact that Lockwood considers the words the girl has spoken to be a product of his own thoughts indicates that he believes this encounter to be a dream, and that he believes the girl to exist only inside his own**

head. Further to this, given that he had heard the name 'Catherine Earnshaw' used more frequently than 'Catherine Linton,' he is curious as to why his mind had put the name Linton into the ghostly girl's mouth.

This is a very tricky question. To many students this line will seem disorientating – why is Lockwood thinking that another character's words are the product of his own thoughts?

To gain the marks, a candidate needs to acknowledge: a) that this quote suggests Lockwood believes this to be a dream; and b) that, prior to this event, he had clearly heard the name Catherine Earnshaw more times than Catherine Linton.

b) '...maintained its tenacious grip, almost maddening me with fear.' [2]

Lockwood, finding himself in the dogged clutches of this girl's hand, experiences such extreme horror that he claims it has taken him to the verge of insanity.

This question is far simpler than the one preceding it. A mark for acknowledging that the girl's grip is remarkably persistent/forceful, and one for acknowledging that it has taken Lockwood to the brink of insanity.

6. Lines 23-24

Once Lockwood has escaped the girl's grip, what two things does Lockwood do in an attempt to insulate himself from the girl? [2]

a) **Lockwood builds a pyramid of books in order to block the girl from entering.**

b) **Lockwood places his fingers in his ears in order to ward off the sound.**

Again, since they are not asking for a quote, write the answer out properly – though, once again, do not fret if you are using some vocabulary from the passage: this is not an 'in your own words' question.

To score these marks, you need to be making the exact two observations I have made above.

7. Lines 28-29

At lines 28-29 it says the following: "It is twenty years,' mourned the voice: 'twenty years. I've been a waif for twenty years!' Explain what you think this could mean. [3]

A waif is a word used to described a child who has been cast away, abandoned, or even made homeless. This quote suggests it has been twenty years since this ghostly girl (or perhaps the person she once was) had been cast away, and that she has been existing as a castaway ever since (seemingly in a state of eternal youth). The tone of her voice suggests this to be a tragic set of circumstances.

This is a tricky question, if only because the word waif will be unfamiliar to a number of candidates, yet is key to scoring the first of the three marks. Arguably, though, the fact the girl earlier says she has returned home may be enough to infer the meaning. Be alert to details, and do have a go at deducing definitions when doing so is essential to scoring marks.

The second mark is for acknowledging that this girl – given the tension between her youthful looks and her twenty years of wandering – must be some kind of supernatural/ghostly entity. The third mark is for acknowledging the tragic import of her words.

8. Lines 28-32

In your own words, explain why Lockwood yells at line 32. [2]

Lockwood's yell appears to be triggered by the girl's attempt to cast the pyramid of books aside, and thus, presumably, gain entry. It seems as though the scream was both his next best defence mechanism in the face of sudden physical paralysis, but also a vocalisation of his horror at having been rendered paralysed.

For both marks, you need to include both the girl's attempt to shove the books, and the fact that the yell also occurred as a result of his physical paralysis.

9. Lines 39-41

Between lines 39-41, what reason does Lockwood give for making his presence known to Heathcliff? [2]

Lockwood announces his presence because he suspects that Heathcliff will continue searching the room. Implicit here is Lockwood's belief that, if Heathcliff continues searching, he will inevitably find Lockwood, thereby rendering any attempt to keep silent on Lockwood's part futile.

You will only score one mark if you just mention the fact that Lockwood believes that Heathcliff will continue looking. To score both marks, you need to demonstrate an understanding that Lockwood is insinuating that if Heathcliff continues looking, he will find Lockwood either way, thus Lockwood might as well give himself up.

10. Lines 42-45

How do we know that Heathcliff is in a state of high anxiety after Lockwood opens the panels? Looking at lines 42-45, find two phrases that tell you this. [4]

a) **'...startled him like an electric shock: the light leaped from his hold.**

b) **'...his agitation was so extreme that he could hardly pick it up.'**

The phrase 'as white as the wall behind him' does not work, because this is a description of Heathcliff before the panels have been opened.

Note that a phrase does not need to be a full sentence. Use an ellipsis (three dots in a row) to indicate that it is part of a longer sentence.

11. Lines 46-47

At lines 46-47, Lockwood asserts that he was: 'desirous to spare him the humiliation of exposing his cowardice further.' What does this mean? [2]

Lockwood, when he refers to Heathcliff's cowardice, is alluding to the frazzled nerves Heathcliff has already exhibited through his physical agitation.[1] Lockwood deems these physical signs of stress to be embarrassing and humiliating displays of weakness. Lockwood is keen to make his presence known, since he believes that, once Heathcliff knows that he is not alone, he will make a greater effort to conceal his fear.

To score the first mark, you need to make the link between Heathcliff's physical jitters to Lockwood's assessment that Heathcliff is exhibiting cowardice. To score the second, you need to understand that Lockwood is trying to save Heathcliff from embarrassing himself further.

12. Using the whole passage, explain how the writer uses language to make this sequence terrifying. Use short quotations to support your answer. [8]

A key method the writer uses to make this sequence terrifying for the reader is, quite simply, by vividly exploring Lockwood's own sensations of terror, which encourages the reader to vicariously feel these sensations, too. Lockwood's own terror is referenced time and again: for instance, when the girl/Catherine pushes the books, Lockwood not only alliteratively references his 'frenzy of fright,' but also catalogues his physical signifiers of terror: 'I... could not stir a limb.' The word 'stir' is particularly effective here, since it is a word that can also be used as a synonym for waking up. As a result, by writing that he 'could not stir,' the implication is that Lockwood (and, vicariously, the reader) is trapped in his state of nightmare-like fear.

Vicarious terror is also achieved through Heathcliff's horror. The visceral simile, noting how the sound of the oak 'startled [Heathcliff] like an electric shock,' and the full-body distress it evokes, acts as a shock to the reader, too.

Terror is also conjured in the passage through depictions of violence. The girl/Catherine deploys a violently harsh grip as she seizes Lockwood: Lockwood talks of 'struggling... to disengage' himself, the verb 'struggling' evocative of prey caught in a trap. Lockwood, in response, then escalates the violence: he describes how he 'rubbed' the ghost's wrists 'to and fro' – these monosyllabic words almost mimicking the short, sharp sawing motion – and observes how the blood 'ran down and soaked the bedclothes,' the excessive blood mirroring the excessive violence. When the 'pile of books moved as if thrust,' the word 'thrust' is reminiscent of the thrust and parry of a sword fight, insinuating that the girl/Catherine is engaging in offensive action. Taken together, these descriptions of physical violence create a sense of physical danger, and are a powerful engine for generating terror.

The passage also strikes terror in the reader through uncertainty – especially the uncertainty surrounding Catherine. For starters, her appearance is terrifyingly uncertain. Lockwood may feel her 'little, ice-cold hand,' and seems to have a visual on the bleeding wrist; however, the hand seems almost disembodied.[2] Indeed, while Lockwood gets a

glimpse at the girl's face, the details he sees are paltry: he observes that he 'discerned, obscurely, a child's face' – yet not only is the face seemingly as disembodied as the hand, but the word 'obscurely' places emphasis on the inadequacy of Lockwood's vision. However, the uncertainty surrounding Catherine are even more profound, because doubts are cast as to whether she even exists at all. Lockwood, at the passage's close, describes the incident as a 'frightful nightmare.' One might argue that what makes this passage truly a 'frightful nightmare' is the language of uncertainty regarding whether the incident even took place.

Just as in the previous paper of this kind, the final question takes the form of a mini essay that is asking us to focus on how the author uses language.

Here is the plan I put together before writing the above:

- Vivid descriptions of horror (both Lockwood's and Heathcliff's) – a prompt for reader to experience it vicariously.
- Acrimony of the dialogue.
- Depictions of violence.
- Uncertainty surrounding the girl's physical appearance, and the event as a whole

As you can see, once I started writing, I realised that the plan was likely too long, so I decided to axe my discussion of the acrimonious dialogue that takes place between Lockwood and Catherine – even though this discussion would certainly have been relevant, and, if I had pursued it at the expense of one of the themes above, would likely still have won me the marks. When it comes to these mini essays, there are often many ways to skin the cat.

Once again, I am adding an extra paragraph – one that deals with yet another theme – in order to demonstrate other ways one might have gone about scoring marks here:

The writer inspires terror in part through establishing a sense of initial calm, which then makes the ensuing drama all the more horrifying. The relatively unthreatening nature of the opening paragraph lulls the reader into a false sense of security: what Lockwood believes to be 'the fir-bough' makes a 'teasing' sound – the word 'teasing' casting it as a harmless annoyance. Indeed, although the weather conditions ('gusty wind' and 'driving snow') are arguably threatening, there is an implicit

cosiness from being removed from the elements. As a result of this use of language to minimise a sense of threat, the writer is able to heighten the terror of the proceeding action.

Speculative & Creative Papers

Note: This style of paper is definitely the most idiosyncratic of the bunch; and although a small handful of its questions resemble those we have seen elsewhere, many of its questions are very much distinct. Unlike the other papers, the Speculative and Creative Paper frequently requires the candidate to directly proffer their opinions, make personal judgements, and exercise their powers of imagination.

For those who are more analytically minded, this style of paper can be the most tricky. On the other hand, it also offers many more opportunities for creativity and flair.

Both of the Speculative & Creative papers I've included here are out of a total of forty-one marks.

Paper Seven: The System of Doctor Tarr and Professor Feather

SPECULATIVE & CREATIVE PAPER; DEVILISH; 45 MINUTES

In this passage, set in the nineteenth century, an unnamed narrator visits a lunatic asylum in the south of France.

---

1 During the autumn of 18--, while on a tour through the extreme southern provinces of France, my route led me within a few miles of a certain *Maison de Santé* or private mad-house, about which I had heard much in Paris from my medical friends. As I had never visited a place of the kind, I thought the opportunity too good to be lost;
5 and so proposed to my travelling companion (a gentleman with whom I had made casual acquaintance a few days before) that we should turn aside, for an hour or so, and look through the establishment. To this he objected -- pleading haste in the first place, and, in the second, a very usual horror at the sight of a lunatic. He begged me, however, not to let any mere courtesy towards himself interfere with the gratification
10 of my curiosity, and said that he would ride on leisurely, so that I might overtake him during the day, or, at all events, during the next. As he bade me good-bye, I bethought me that there might be some difficulty in obtaining access to the premises, and mentioned my fears on this point. He replied that, in fact, unless I had personal knowledge of the superintendent, Monsieur Maillard, or some credential in the way
15 of a letter, a difficulty might be found to exist, as the regulations of these private mad-houses were more rigid than the public hospital laws. For himself, he added, he had, some years since, made the acquaintance of Maillard, and would so far assist me as to ride up to the door and introduce me; although his feelings on the subject of lunacy would not permit of his entering the house.

20 I thanked him, and, turning from the main road, we entered a grass-grown by-path, which, in half an hour, nearly lost itself in a dense forest, clothing the base of a mountain. Through this dank and gloomy wood we rode some two miles, when the *Maison de Santé* came in view. It was a fantastic *château*, much dilapidated, and indeed scarcely tenantable through age and neglect. Its aspect inspired me with absolute 25 dread, and, checking my horse, I half resolved to turn back. I soon, however, grew ashamed of my weakness, and proceeded.

As we rode up to the gate-way, I perceived it slightly open, and the visage of a man peering through. In an instant afterward, this man came forth, accosted my companion by name, shook him cordially by the hand, and begged him to alight. It 30 was Monsieur Maillard himself. He was a portly, fine-looking gentleman of the old school, with a polished manner, and a certain air of gravity, dignity, and authority which was very impressive.

My friend, having presented me, mentioned my desire to inspect the establishment, and received Monsieur Maillard's assurance that he would show me all attention, 35 now took leave, and I saw him no more.

When he had gone, the superintendent ushered me into a small and exceedingly neat parlor, containing, among other indications of refined taste, many books, drawings, pots of flowers, and musical instruments. A cheerful fire blazed upon the hearth. At a piano, singing an aria from Bellini, sat a young and very beautiful woman, who, at my 40 entrance, paused in her song, and received me with graceful courtesy. Her voice was low, and her whole manner subdued. I thought, too, that I perceived the traces of sorrow in her countenance, which was excessively, although to my taste, not unpleasingly, pale. She was attired in deep mourning, and excited in my bosom a feeling of mingled respect, interest, and admiration.

45 I had heard, at Paris, that the institution of Monsieur Maillard was managed upon what is vulgarly termed the "system of soothing" -- that all punishments were avoided -- that even confinement was seldom resorted to -- that the patients, while secretly watched, were left much apparent liberty, and that most of them were permitted to roam about the house and grounds in the ordinary apparel of persons in right mind.

50 Keeping these impressions in view, I was cautious in what I said before the young lady; for I could not be sure that she was sane; and, in fact, there was a certain restless brilliancy about her eyes which half led me to imagine she was not. I confined my remarks, therefore, to general topics, and to such as I thought would not be displeasing or exciting even to a lunatic. She replied in a perfectly rational manner to 55 all that I said; and even her original observations were marked with the soundest good sense, but a long acquaintance with the metaphysics of mania, had taught me to put no faith in such evidence of sanity, and I continued to practise, throughout the interview, the caution with which I commenced it.

Presently a smart footman in livery brought in a tray with fruit, wine, and other
60 refreshments, of which I partook, the lady soon afterward leaving the room. As she departed I turned my eyes in an inquiring manner toward my host.

"No," he said, "oh, no — a member of my family — my niece, and a most accomplished woman." "I beg a thousand pardons for the suspicion," I replied, "but of course you will know how to excuse me. The excellent administration of your affairs
65 here is well understood in Paris, and I thought it just possible, you know—

"Yes, yes — say no more — or rather it is myself who should thank you for the commendable prudence you have displayed."

An extract from Edgar Allan Poe's 'The System of Dr Feather and Professor Tarr'

---

1. The passage describes a mental health institution from over one hundred years ago. Describe THREE ways you think it might differ from a modern-day mental health institution? [3]

2. What do you think that the writer means when he refers to the travelling companion's 'very usual horror at the sight of a lunatic.' (line 8)? [4]

3. The word 'dilapidated' come from the Latin word 'dilapidare,' which means to scatter. What do you think the writer means when he describes the building as 'dilapidated'? [4]

4. Re-read the description of Monsieur Maillard in lines 27 ('As we rode…') to 32 ('...very impressive'). Choose a phrase from these lines that you think describes Monsieur Maillard particularly well and explain why you chose it. [6]

5. What types of books and drawings do you think might be in the 'parlor' that the narrator enters at lines 36-37? [8]

6. Re-read the description of the system of soothing in lines 45 ('I had heard…') to 49 ('... right mind'). What do the writer's choice of words in these lines suggest about the narrator's feelings towards the system of soothing? [4]

7. Look at the portrayal of the woman in lines 38 ('At a piano, singing an aria') to 58 ('…with which I commenced it'). Do you find it surprising that the narrator suspects she might be insane? Give reasons for your answer. [7]

8. Do you think that Monsieur Maillard seems like a good superintendant for the Maison de Santé? Give reasons for your answer, using details from the passage. [5]

Paper Seven: Model Answers & Guidance

1. The passage describes a mental health institution from over one hundred years ago. Describe THREE ways you think it might differ from a modern-day mental health institution? [3]

a) Whereas this institution operates out of a rundown castle, one would expect that a modern-day institution would likely operate from a custom-built building, and efforts would be made to keep the building up to code.

b) Whereas there are no security checks at Maison de Santé as the narrator enters, one might expect a modern-day mental health institution to have at least some rudimentary security procedures for visitors.

c) The interior design of Maison de Santé – with its piano and open fire – is far more lavish than one would expect to find in a modern-day mental health institution. A modern-day institution, while perhaps still comfortable, would likely have a far more clinical aesthetic.

The examiners will not be consulting a list of observations candidates might make. Rather, the examiner is asking you to take a good look at the setting the narrator has entered, and to identify aspects that *our* society would find odd or out of place. So long as your observations are convincing and sensible, you will secure the marks.

2. What do you think that the writer means when he refers to the travelling companion's 'very usual horror at the sight of a lunatic.' (line 8)? [4]

The writer with this comment is suggesting that the narrator feels as though experiencing horror when encountering an insane individual – as his travelling companion apparently does – is completely understandable and relatable. However, the word 'usual,' aside from suggesting that the companion's reaction is to be expected, also suggests that such a reaction is commonplace: it is more usual than not to feel that way.

This question is more reminiscent of those we have seen in other papers.

This paper is designating more marks than other papers do for this style of question, but do not be thrown off by this – just remember that any given exam paper you encounter is often unique to the school you are applying for, and, as a result, the small discrepancy in marks does not necessarily mean you have to answer the question in a wholly different way.

Two marks are likely to be set aside for demonstrating you understand the content of quote – that the writer is communicating that the narrator's companion experiences horror when encountering mentally unstable individuals, and that the narrator considers this tendency both commonplace and understandable. The other two marks will for expressing yourself with sophistication and flair.

3. The word 'dilapidated' come from the Latin word 'dilapidare,' which means to scatter. What do you think the writer means when he describes the building as 'dilapidated'? [4]

First and foremost, the writer is likely trying to convey with the word 'dilapidated' that the building is in a state of extreme disrepair that has been wrought by age: it is in ruins, a shadow of what it once was. However, the notion of scatter feeds into, and augments, this sense of the building being in ruin: it is as if to say that the constituent parts of the chateau, which were once in perfect order, have now been metaphorically (and perhaps, up to a point, literally) scattered and thrown into relative chaos.

If the exam paper is giving you an extra titbit – like, for instance, this information about a word's Latin etymology – the safe thing to do, even if you are not told explicitly to do so, is to work it into your answer.[1]

Above, I am scoring two marks for relaying my understanding of the generally accepted definition of dilapidated as run-down and in a state of disrepair. However, the next two marks are for reflecting on how the etymology of the word offers further insight into the author's use of vocabulary.

4. Re-read the description of Monsieur Maillard in lines 27 ('As we rode...") to 32 ('...very impressive'). Choose a phrase from these lines that you think describes Monsieur Maillard particularly well and explain why you chose it. [6]

> **I feel as though the observation that he was a 'gentleman of the old-school' is a particularly apt phrase to describe Maillard. The expression 'old-school' evokes a traditionalism that is borne out in Maillard's aesthetic tastes – his institution operates from a Gothic castle that, even for the nineteenth century, has a distinctly anachronistic quality, and his parlour also harks to an old-world glamour.[2] Indeed, even though he appears to be an innovator (as opposed to a traditionalist) with his 'system of soothing,' the fact he appears to be an older man is in keeping with an old-school worldview, which elevates patriarchal figures, and casts them as those who have the latitude to innovate in the first place.[3] Certainly, that he is a 'gentleman' also feeds into this interpretation of Maillard, for a gentleman in the Victorian era was shorthand for someone who subscribed to 'old-school' codes of decorum.**

Of course it is important here to pick out a relevant quote. However, more important than the quote is the explanation of why you think the phrase you have picked is particularly apt.

Notice how I use 'old school' not only to shed light on Maillard's artistic tastes, but also on his role in society at large. Notice, also, how at the end of my answer I give a little bit of analysis on the word 'gentleman' – I want to make sure I am offering analysis on the entirety of the quote I have picked out, including the bits that I consider less juicy.

The quote you pick really should not be more than, say, six words. If you are selective with your choice, this will be more than enough to work with.

5. What types of books and drawings do you think might be in the 'parlor' that the narrator enters at lines 36-37? [8]

First and foremost, given the centrality of religion in European life during the nineteenth century, one would expect to find a bible in such a parlour. One would imagine, however, that scientific reference books might predominate. In particular, one might expect to see books on phrenology – the (now discredited) study of how skull shapes influence behaviour, and, depending when exactly this event takes place (the year is redacted), perhaps books by Cesare Lombroso, who attempted to draw connections between skull shapes and criminal behaviour.[4] Indeed, there may also be drawings relating to phrenology – for instance, skulls and their measurements – on the wall.

Beyond scientific books, one would also expect touchstone references books, such as a dictionary, to be present. There could also perhaps be a few books relating to history and philosophy. A book by the eighteenth century philosopher, Jean-Jacques Rousseau, might be particularly at home in an institution of this kind: not only was he French, but his work dealt with the relationship between individuals and society.

Insofar as the drawings are concerned, one might imagine there to be drawings by some of *Maison de Santé* inmates; after all, given the 'system of soothing,' and the bent towards artistry hinted at by the instruments, it could be part of their policy to encourage the inmates to engage in drawing as an artistic pursuit. One might also imagine that there could be drawings that are explicitly intended to induce calm in those who might set eyes on them, given that the inmates could occasionally frequent the room. In my mind's eye, there are also hand-drawn maps of the area of southern France in which the chateau is situated.

This is perhaps the trickiest question in this paper, and the trickiest style of question you will likely encounter during your 11+ comprehension exams as a whole. The question is asking you to speculate; and whereas you might expect it to be worth just a couple of marks, it is in fact the highest scoring question on the paper.

Again, the examiner will not have a mark scheme containing all the "acceptable" answers. After all, this question is explicitly encouraging creativity.

And yet, while this question is encouraging creativity, that does not mean you should be putting in absurd answers. We have some parameters within which to work: we know that the institution is dedicated to housing the mentally ill; that the story is set in the nineteenth century France; that, given the musical instruments, Maillard likely has at least some interest in the arts; and that, given the architecture of the chateau,

Maillard likely has some interest in the Gothic. Any answers that can be reasonably extrapolated from these parameters will be credited. Perhaps he also had books on the French Revolution? Perhaps he had drawings that were not calming, but instead depicted buildings that were just as dilapidated as the chateau? The possibilities are endless.

6. Re-read the description of the system of soothing in lines 45 ('I had heard ...) to 49 ('... right mind'). What do the writer's choice of words in these lines suggest about the narrator's feelings towards the system of soothing? [4]

A key word the writer puts in the narrator's mouth is the adverb 'vulgarly,' which is in fact the way the narrator describes the term 'system of soothing' itself – the phrase Parisians use to describe Maillard's method. The word reveals that the narrator in fact has a great deal of respect and reverence for the system of soothing – so much so that he feels as though it warrants a more grandiose, or perhaps more subtle, name. When the narrator observes that 'even confinement was seldom resorted to,' the word 'even' suggests incredulity and astonishment at what he perceives to be the system's revolutionary nature. Phrases such as 'secretly watched' and 'apparent liberty' suggest an appreciation for the system's subtlety: he construes the liberty the patients enjoy as in fact an artfully designed illusion.

To score four marks, you would want to engage in close analysis of at least two separate words / phrases. Since my analysis of the word 'vulgarly' was so much meatier than my analysis of the phrase 'even confinement was seldom resorted to,' I decided to add one extra comment on 'secretly watched' and 'apparent liberty' to ensure I was not losing a mark for my brevity.

7. Look at the portrayal of the woman in lines 38 ('At a piano, singing an aria') to 58 ('…with which I commenced it'). Do you find it surprising that the narrator suspects she might be insane? Give reasons for your answer. [7]

In my view, perhaps the most compelling reason one might find it surprising that the narrator suspects the woman might be insane is the rational and coherent way in which she engaged in conversation. It is true that the narrator intentionally tailored the conversation to topics he believed 'would not be displeasing or exciting' to 'a lunatic' – nevertheless, not only were her answers 'perfectly rational,' but it seems that, when she initiated conversation, she also exhibited 'the soundest good sense.' Beyond her coherency, there are other factors that should

have reasonably assuaged the narrator's suspicions: for instance, the woman's acknowledgement of social niceties (she received the narrator 'with a graceful curtsey,') and the implicit focus that her ability to sing an 'aria from Bellini' suggests.

Moreover, a part of me thinks that Maillard would have surely have given the narrator prior warning that the woman was not sound of mind.

However, despite all of the above, there are certainly also compelling reasons to be unsurprised by the narrator's suspicions. Chief among them is the 'system of soothing,' which makes it entirely plausible that the woman might be one of Maillard's patients. More subtle factors also raise eyebrows. The way she dresses – she is 'attired in deep mourning' – is arguably a red flag, especially since there are no obvious reasons for such attire – and so too, arguably, is the 'certain restless brilliancy in her eyes.' Also very compelling is the narrator's logic that one must not take coherency of conversation as 'evidence of sanity,' since insanity can manifest in other ways.

Overall, especially given the system of soothing, I do not find it surprising that the narrator should at the very least entertain suspicions regarding the woman's mental state, and that he has chosen to put limited store by her coherency of conversation as a sign of sanity.

The 'Do you find X surprising?' is another classic question in the Creative and Speculative Paper. The secret here is to explore both sides of the argument in depth (and with quotations!), and then (and this is important) come to a verdict. It usually does not matter which side you pick in the end. The important thing is that you can justify your choice.

You will notice that often when answering comprehension questions I try and avoid using the word 'I,' because I generally think it is more scholarly to avoid it, and to say things like: 'one may argue' or 'one might observe.' However, this sort of question is explicitly asking us to give our opinion, so using 'I' is essential (indeed, the Creative and Speculative Paper is, as a whole, far more personal than the others, and encourages this personalised response).

Here is the plan I quickly threw together before I started writing:

- Surprising: Singing, curtseying with poise; firm handle on the conversation. The overall impression the narrator draws is one of respect and admiration. Also, one would surely expect Maillard to give him prior warning?

- Unsurprising: The system of soothing boosts the likelihood of patients wandering around. The way she dresses, and her manner / look in her eyes. One can only infer so much from social poise.
- Overall not surprising, given system of soothing.

8. Do you think that Monsieur Maillard seems like a good superintendant for the Maison de Santé? Give reasons for your answer, using details from the passage. [5]

At the start of the passage, the narrator notes that he 'had heard much, in Paris' about Maison de Santé from his medical friends. This suggests that Maillard has been running the Maison in an innovative way that is worthy of note; and insofar as innovation might be considered a boon, this arguably suggests he is a good superintendant. A firmer indication of his virtues could be inferred from the way he greets the narrator's friend. One might imagine the warmth and hospitality he exhibits (he 'shook [the friend] cordially by hand' and 'begged him to alight') to be something he transfers to his professional work. It seems wise to me, also, to take the narrator's own impressions of Maillard – namely, Maillard's 'air of gravity, dignity and authority' – as at least a partial indication of Maillard's professionalism.

However, while there are factors to suggest he is a good superintendant, there are other signs that seem to me less rosy. For one thing, it seems remarkable that he has allowed the narrator to bypass the visitors' vetting process – that is, 'some credential in the way of a letter.' For another, the fact that he neglects to tell the narrator beforehand whether the singer is of sound mind smacks of unprofessionalism. In my view, it seems entirely possible – perhaps even likely – that the narrator has been taken in by Maillard's 'polished manner,' and that in fact Maillard is an individual whose outward polish masks a lack of competency. Indeed, my overall feeling is that he is likely not a good superintendant; and while I have observed that the talk he generates in Paris *could* be a sign of his pre-eminence, it seems far more likely that to me it is an indication of his notoriety.[5]

This question is fairly similar to the one beforehand, yet is asking us to judge a character rather than a situation / a character's opinion.

Again, it is important to discuss both sides of the argument while drawing on quotations from the passage, and then to make a well-reasoned personal verdict. However, since this question is worth fewer marks than the one beforehand, you will want to make it slightly shorter and sharper.

Here is the brief plan I put together prior to writing the above:

- Good superintendant: His reputation precedes him, which may bode well. His warm greeting of the narrator's friend suggests empathetic traits. The narrator is impressed by Maillard.
- Bad superintendant: Negligently waives vetting process for narrator. Neglects to inform narrator whether the woman is sound of mind. Outward polish over substance.
- Overall: a bag superintendant – in fact, reputation in Paris more likely a sign of his notoriety than a tick in his favour.

Paper Eight: Three Lives

SPECULATIVE & CREATIVE PAPER; DEVILISH; 45 MINUTES

This passage is taken from a novel set in the late 1890s / early 1900s, and takes place in a fictional town on the east coast of America. This passage discusses the various women who worked for Miss Mathilda.

---

1 For five years Anna managed the little house for Miss Mathilda. In these five years there were four different under servants.

The one that came first was a pretty, cheerful irish girl. Anna took her with a doubting mind. Lizzie was an obedient, happy servant, and Anna began to have a
5 little faith. This was not for long. The pretty, cheerful Lizzie disappeared one day without her notice and with all her baggage and returned no more.

This pretty, cheerful Lizzie was succeeded by a melancholy Molly.

Molly was born in America, of german parents. All her people had been long dead or gone away. Molly had always been alone. She was a tall, dark, sallow, thin-haired
10 creature, and she was always troubled with a cough, and she had a bad temper, and always said ugly dreadful swear words.

Anna found all this very hard to bear, but she kept Molly a long time out of kindness. The kitchen was constantly a battle-ground. Anna scolded and Molly swore strange oaths, and then Miss Mathilda would shut her door hard to show that she could hear
15 it all.

At last Anna had to give it up. "Please Miss Mathilda won't you speak to Molly," Anna said, "I can't do a thing with her. I scold her, and she don't seem to hear and then she swears so that she scares me. She loves you Miss Mathilda, and you scold her please once."

20 "But Anna," cried poor Miss Mathilda, "I don't want to," and that large, cheerful, but faint hearted woman looked all aghast at such a prospect. "But you must, please Miss Mathilda!" Anna said.

Miss Mathilda never wanted to do any scolding. "But you must please

Miss Mathilda," Anna said.

25 Miss Mathilda every day put off the scolding, hoping always that Anna would learn to manage Molly better. It never did get better and at last Miss Mathilda saw that the scolding simply had to be.

It was agreed between the good Anna and her Miss Mathilda that Anna should be away when Molly would be scolded. The next evening that it was Anna's evening out,
30 Miss Mathilda faced her task and went down into the kitchen.

Molly was sitting in the little kitchen leaning her elbows on the table. She was a tall, thin, sallow girl, aged twenty-three, by nature slatternly and careless but trained by Anna into superficial neatness. Her drab striped cotton dress and gray black checked apron increased the length and sadness of her melancholy figure.

35 "Oh, Lord!" groaned Miss Mathilda to herself as she approached her.

"Molly, I want to speak to you about your behaviour to Anna!", here

Molly dropped her head still lower on her arms and began to cry.

"Oh! Oh!" groaned Miss Mathilda.

"It's all Miss Annie's fault, all of it," Molly said at last, in a trembling voice, "I do my
40 best."

"I know Anna is often hard to please," began Miss Mathilda, with a twinge of mischief, and then she sobered herself to her task, "but you must remember, Molly, she means it for your good and she is really very kind to you."

"I don't want her kindness," Molly cried, "I wish you would tell me what to do, Miss
45 Mathilda, and then I would be all right. I hate Miss Annie."

"This will never do Molly," Miss Mathilda said sternly, in her deepest, firmest tones, "Anna is the head of the kitchen and you must either obey her or leave."

"I don't want to leave you," whimpered melancholy Molly. "Well Molly then try and

do better," answered Miss Mathilda, keeping a good stern front, and backing quickly
50 from the kitchen.

"Oh! Oh!" groaned Miss Mathilda, as she went back up the stairs.

Miss Mathilda's attempt to make peace between the constantly contending women in the kitchen had no real effect. They were very soon as bitter as before.

At last it was decided that Molly was to go away. Molly went away to work in a
55 factory in the town, and she went to live with an old woman in the slums, a very bad old woman Anna said.

Anna was never easy in her mind about the fate of Molly. Sometimes she would see or hear of her. Molly was not well, her cough was worse, and the old woman really was a bad one.

An extract from Gertrude Stein's *Three Lives*

---

1. The passage details the relationship between women, all of whom have a professional relationship with each other. Describe THREE ways in which their relationships differ from what you might expect. [3]

2. Re-read the description of Lizzie in lines 3 ('The one that came first ...) to 6 ('... returned no more'). What do the writer's choice of words in these lines suggest about Anna's feelings towards Lizzie? [4]

3. What do you think might have caused Lizzie to have left Mathilda's employ after such a short spell? [8]

4. The word 'melancholy' comes from the Greek word 'melankholia' which means 'black bile.' What do you think the writer means when she describes Molly as 'melancholy? [4]

5. Re-read the description of Molly in lines 31 ('Molly was sitting...") to 34 ('...melancholy figure'). Choose a phrase from these lines that you think describes Molly particularly well and explain why you chose it. **(Do not choose a phrase containing the word 'Melancholy.')** [6]

6. What do you think the writer means when she refers to Miss Mathilda's 'twinge of mischief.' (lines 41-42)? [4]

7. Look at the portrayal of Mathilda in lines 35 ('"O Lord...') to 51 ('...back up the stairs'). Based on this portrayal, do you find it surprising that Molly wishes to stay in Mathilda's employ? Give reasons for your answer. [7]

8. Do you think that Anna seems like a good boss? Give reasons for your answer, using details from the passage. [5]

Paper Eight: Model Answers & Guidance

1. The passage details the relationship between women, all of whom have a professional relationship with each other. Describe THREE ways in which their relationships differ from what you might expect. [3]

> **a) Given that she is the employer, one would expect Mathilda to exercise power over Anna, and to instruct Anna on how she ought to handle Molly. However, it instead appears as if it is Anna who has power over Mathilda, and instructs her on what to do.**
>
> **b) Whereas one would expect Molly to keep her emotions out of her interactions with Mathilda, her employer, she does the reverse, exhibiting emotional entanglement with Mathilda, and openly voicing resentment about her superior (Anna).**
>
> **c) Given Molly's animosity towards Anna, one might expect Anna to reciprocate in kind. Instead, Anna appears to worry about Molly, even after she leaves Mathilda's employ.**

Again, the trick here is to go a step beyond merely picking up on details – you also need to intelligently weigh what you see here against your own expectations and experiences. You will be credited for any sensible argument.

2. Re-read the description of Lizzie in lines 3 ('The one that came first ...) to 6 ('...

returned no more'). What do the writer's choice of words in these lines suggest about Anna's feelings towards Lizzie? [4]

That Anna had 'a doubting mind' when first taking Lizzie on suggests that she had reservations regarding Lizzie's suitability for the position of under-servant. Although it appears as though Anna somewhat warmed to Lizzie – the phrase 'obedient, happy servant,' given the free indirect style, appears to be Anna's own assessment – she never fully overcame her reservations. Indeed, even at this high point, Anna never had anything more than a slither of faith ('a little faith') in Lizzie.

There are three key quotes you need to be picking up on here, and each one you include and properly explain will score you a mark. The fourth mark will be awarded for the maturity and sophistication of your answer as a whole.

3. What do you think might have caused Lizzie to have left Mathilda's employ after such a short spell? [8]

Perhaps Lizzie left as a result of her home life, which – as it was for many poorer, working class women at the turn of the nineteenth century – might've been characterised by tumult. This could have manifested in any number of ways, but plausible eventualities might include having suddenly fallen pregnant; having been coerced into leaving the job by an abusive partner; or being required to care to a sick family member. Indeed, it is entirely possible that she grew sick herself; after all, we know Molly developed a cough, so it is plausible that Lizzie might have fallen sick, too.

A rosier reason for Lizzie's departure may have simply been that she had found more favourable employment elsewhere – employment that was either less strenuous, or offered better pay. Equally, it might have been the case that Lizzie left not to work in a conventional sense, but to pursue a different calling altogether. Perhaps she joined the suffragette, as one of their few working class members, since the movement was gathering steam at the turn of the twentieth century.

Of course, it may have been the case that she left not to pursue something else, but because, despite her positive demeanour, she was having a hard time getting along with Anna. We know that Molly had a hard time with Anna, and that Anna always harboured reservations about Lizzie. Moreover, that Anna oversaw four under-servants in all

suggests that Molly was not alone in finding Anna tough to work for. As a result of all this, it is entirely possible that Lizzie left due to discomfort with her superior. There may have even been some other cause of discomfort at the work place – perhaps a run-in with a neighbour, or an assault – that made Lizzie feel as though her position at Mathilda's house was untenable.

This is another of these fiendish speculative questions – it seems innocuous enough, but then you realise there are eight marks in play.

Again, lean into the creativity this style of question invites. We know that Lizzie is a working class woman living at the turn of the twentieth century, that she is based in a small town on the east coast of America, and that she is seemingly a positive, can-do personality. So long as the reasons you proffer do not clash terribly with these details, you have free rein.

4. The word 'melancholy' comes from the Greek word 'melankholia' which means 'black bile.' What do you think the writer means when she describes Molly as 'melancholy? [4]

On the most basic level, the writer is trying to convey a state of persistent sadness and depression when describing Molly with the word 'melancholy' – indeed, the writer is not trying to convey a momentary blip of sadness, but a depression that is more intrinsic to her personality. The idea of black bile coheres with this notion. The blackness is a metaphoric one: it refers to a darkness of mood. Bile, on the other hand, used to be considered by doctors as the fluid responsible for feelings of depression.

You will secure two marks for demonstrating that melancholy is a word that encompasses a sense of profound sadness and depression. The third mark is for understanding that the idea of blackness in the word's etymology refers to a metaphorical blackness/darkness of mind.

The fourth mark is undoubtedly the trickiest, and it is for explaining how 'bile' adds to our understanding of the word melancholy (I suspect some students simply will not know what it means). However, if you do find yourself stumped about one element of a question, keep a cool head and don't let it stop you giving an answer. After all, you can clearly still score three of the four marks without knowing what bile means.

5. Re-read the description of Molly in lines 31 ('Molly was sitting...") to 34 ('...melancholy figure'). Choose a phrase from these lines that you think describes Molly particularly well and explain why you chose it. (Do not choose a phrase containing the word 'Melancholy.') [6]

A phrase that seems a particularly apt descriptor of Molly is the observation that she was 'by nature slatternly and careless.' 'Slatternly' not only conjures up a dishevelled, even dirty, aesthetic, but also hints at a laxness in behaviour that is the root cause of the dishevelment. The word itself – an ictus, followed by two unstressed syllables – trails off, as if mimicking this laxness.[1] 'Careless' also seems to explain her untidy demeanour – she does not take care of herself – yet also captures a slapdash attitude in her interactions with the world at large. This seems to prefigure her poor health, since poor health is the logical outcome for an individual who moves through the world with a habitual lack of care.

That Molly is these things 'by nature' is particularly telling: they are traits that are encoded in her, not habits she has learned; and while Anna may be able to help Molly achieve a veneer of presentability, it will always be a veneer.

We have six points in play here, so we need to ensure that we really explore the nuances of the expression we have chosen. Above, I have gone to great lengths to show how the words I've picked out reflect on both Molly's looks *and* behaviour. To score highly, you need to demonstrate how words can have double (and even triple) meanings)

Notice how, in my justification, I also invoke other information the text gives us about the character (on this occasion, the fact she develops a cough) as a means of backing up my argument.

Notice, too, how I have taken time to analyse the expression 'by nature.' Even though I consider this the less 'juicy' part of the phrase I've chosen, I still want to wring out as many marks as possible.

6. What do you think the writer means when she refers to Miss Mathilda's 'twinge of mischief.' (lines 41-42)? [4]

The phrase 'twinge of mischief' appears just as Mathilda is starting to give Molly a talking-to, and Molly is bemoaning her lot. The phrase reveals that Mathilda is in fact taking a perverse pleasure in delivering the scolding, and in hearing Molly's excuses. It could also reveal that

Mathilda feels as though Molly's preceding comment (in which she lays all the blame at Anna's door) gives Mathilda a unique opportunity to play devil's advocate and thus have further fun at Molly's expense – and hints, too, that Mathilda considers the words she has just spoken, in which she describes Anna as 'hard to please,' to be a mischievous understatement. However, that it is only a 'twinge' suggests that Mathilda's mischievous urges are very much under control.

Two marks here are for acknowledging that the phrase suggests Mathilda is taking pleasure in delivering this dressing down, but that the word 'twinge' shows that it was only a flash of pleasure. Two further marks are for placing the quote in context, and exploring the insights it gives us into the specific words Mathilda and Molly had just spoken beforehand.

7. Look at the portrayal of Mathilda in lines 35 ('"O Lord...') to 51 ('...back up the stairs'). Based on this portrayal, do you find it surprising that Molly wishes to stay in Mathilda's employ? Give reasons for your answer. [7]

What I find most surprising about Molly's desire to stay in Mathilda's employ is the fact that, although Molly 'hates' Anna, Mathilda is portrayed as firmly in Anna's corner: Mathilda insists that Anna is 'really very kind' to Molly and that Molly 'must either obey [Anna] or leave.' If Molly truly hates Anna all that much, it is surprising that Mathilda's loyalty to Anna does not alienate Molly. Moreover, Mathilda comes across paradoxically as both frustratingly ineffectual – as exemplified by the refrain of '"Oh! Oh!"' she is heard groaning – yet oddly stern as she dresses Molly down ('keeping a good stern front'). As a result, I feel some surprise that Molly does not feel as though Mathilda is being uncharacteristically – and thus unfairly – stern with her. Finally, one might have thought that Molly would have been able to intuit Mathilda's unkind 'twinge of mischief,' and that this might have sparked in her a desire to leave Mathilda's employ.

On the other hand, it could be argued that, although Mathilda keeps up 'a good stern front,' Molly can in fact intuit a latent empathy in Mathilda – indeed, the way Mathilda groans 'Oh, Lord' as she gears up to the scolding hints to the reader that she would rather spare Molly the ordeal, and perhaps Molly picks up on this, too. Molly perhaps also picks up on the fact that Mathilda would also rather spare *herself* the ordeal of scolding Molly (the 'Oh, Lord' is also arguably a moan of self pity), and has deduced the fact that Anna has put Mathilda up to the scolding – and

this, in turn, would likely have engendered a sense of affinity and camaraderie in Molly towards Mathilda. Mathilda, after all, is yet another individual being made to do something they find uncomfortable by Anna.

On the whole, I do find it surprising that Molly wishes to stay in Mathilda's employ. However, my reason for this is not because Mathilda comes across as a cruel employer (on the contrary, I think on balance she comes across as empathetic), but because Mathilda's loyalties seem ultimately to be to Anna, whom Molly clearly detests.

I am using the same formula I discussed last time we encountered a 'do you find it surprising' style question. First, I have a paragraph (full of evidence from the text) covering the reasons I find Molly's desire to stay surprising; next, I have a paragraph outlining my reasons for finding this not so surprising. Finally, I offer my personal verdict.

Look at it this way: your 'for' and 'against' paragraphs are both worth three marks apiece. And to avoid losing marks, you need to ensure that both of these paragraphs contain at least a couple of convincing reasons, as well as relevant quotes from the text. The final mark is for offering a well-reasoned final verdict; and make sure to use the word 'I' – after all, they are asking for your personal opinion.

Here's a short plan I put together before I started writing.

- Surprising: Mathilda's loyalty is to Anna, not Molly; Mathilda is uncharacteristically stern with Molly; shouldn't Molly to pick up on Mathilda's pleasure in scolding?
- Unsurprising: Perhaps Molly intuits Mathilda's empathy, and the fact that Anna put Mathilda up to the scolding? Perhaps Molly feels camaraderie with Mathilda, since both put upon by Anna?
- Ultimately surprising, given degree to which Mathilda's loyalties are aligned to Anna.

8. Do you think that Anna seems like a good boss? Give reasons for your answer, using details from the passage. [5]

We are told that Anna was frugal with investing faith in Lizzie, and one might argue that a supportive mindset, as opposed to a 'doubting mind,' might be preferable in the workplace. Moreover, the sheer churn of employees under Anna – over 'five years there were four different under

servants' – raises questions regarding her ability to create a healthy working environment. With regards to Molly, it is striking that Anna is unable to bring her subordinate under control – she proves incapable of 'learn[ing] to manage Molly better' – and, instead of trying different approaches, she ropes Mathilda in to fight her battles. That she insists that Mathilda 'scold' Molly, after scolding her repeatedly herself, also points to the limits of Anna's imagination: her approach centres not on the carrot, but on the stick. Unsurprisingly, Anna's scolding by proxy also fails to yield results.

However, while Anna's management style seems flawed, she does not harbour malice for her under-servant. We are told early on that 'she kept Molly a long time out of kindness,' and this kindness is exhibited when, after Molly leaves, Anna maintains an interest in Molly's wellbeing: she was 'never easy... about the fate of Molly.' Moreover, though using Mathilda to fight her battles has been cited as one of Anna's sins, the very fact she has done this (as opposed to simply giving up) can arguably be seen as another indication of underlying kindness – she is looking for excuses to keep Molly on board. One may note, too, that Anna's approach does at least effect some limited positive change in Molly. We are told she is 'trained by Anna into superficial neatness.' While the superficiality is unsatisfying, it still indicates at least some impact.

Overall, I feel that Anna, while perhaps a well-meaning individual, cannot be described as a *good* boss, particularly given her unimaginative dependence on scolding as a management technique.

This answer takes a similar format to the last. Two marks will be rewarded for a well reasoned argument (augmented with quotes) against Anna's efficacy as a boss, and two for a strong argument in her favour. Again, the final mark is reserved for your verdict, which must be backed by a convincing line of reasoning.

Endnotes

Paper One: Model Answers & Guidance

1. The word aesthetic basically refers to how things look.
   If something is tacit, it means that it is not said explicitly , but it is still something we can infer.
2. If you are using your auditory powers, it means you are using your powers of hearing.
3. Uncanny basically means eerie or unsettling. I'm trying to say that it is eerie that Utterson can 'sense' it is Hyde.
4. You can usually spot a interpolated phrase by watching out for a snippet of text that is enclosed on either side by a comma or a dash; and you can tell it is an interpolated phrase because, if you remove it altogether, the sentence will still make sense without it.
5. Put simply, if you are experiencing something vicariously, it means you are experiencing it through someone else. It's a really great word for comprehensions.
6. If something is inexplicable, it is something that can't be explained.
7. If something is implicit, it means it is not explicit – in other words, it has not been said out loud, only hinted at! It is similar to the word tacit.
8. If something is subversive, it is something that undermines authority. To subvert someone is to undermine them.
9. If one thing is akin to another, it means they are similar.
10. Surmise is a very similar word to deduce or infer, and means practically the same thing.
11. Acting with decorum basically means to act politely and with appreciation for social rules and niceties.
12. If you are deferent to someone, it means you are exceedingly respectful to them.
13. If you pay lip service, if means that you say something / do something without really meaning it. I'm trying to say that, while Utterson likes to behave in a way that seems to be polite, really, in many ways, he is not polite!

Paper Two: Model Answers & Guidance

1. If something is ubiquitous, it means that it is everywhere.
2. If you are feeling something acutely, it means you are feeling it intensely.
3. Onomatopoeia is when a word sounds like the thing it refers to. Examples include bang, crash and pop.
4. The minutiae are the small details.
5. Someone's agency is their ability to have control over their actions. I'm suggesting that Chrisfield's anger is so extreme that he is in danger of losing the ability to control himself.
6. Uniformity is when everything looks the same, like these trees.
7. A vacuum is literally a space without any air inside. When you have a vacuum, it is an invitation for air to rush in. I'm using the word here metaphorically: there is an absence of emotion (instead of air), which invites the horror to rush in to fill the empty space!
8. A rubric is kind of like a guideline that others are invited to follow.
9. Viscera refers to internal organs; so a visceral description is one referring, basically, to internal organs – that is, blood and gore!
10. To displace something is to take its place.
    Obliquely means indirectly. So to bring something up obliquely means to bring it up in a round-about way.
11. To be brutalised is to be made brutal by something. Chrisfied has been made brutal by war.
    To be sadistic is to take pleasure in someone else's pain.
12. If something is arbitrary, it means it is without any underpinning logic or reason.
13. A refrain is when a word or a phrase is repeated. A refrain is when a word or a phrase is repeated. A refrain is when a word or a phrase is repeated.

14. Parlance basically means a way of speaking.

Paper Three: Model Answers & Guidance

1. To winnow down a list means to narrow it down.
2. To encroach on something means to intrude on it.
3. Alliteration is when two or more words start with the same letter.
4. Nihilism is the belief that nothing matters and life is meaningless.

   To subjugate someone is to assert control and dominance over them.
5. If something is latent, it means that it exists, but is currently inactive and out of view.
6. You may already know that to trick someone with an illusion is to trick them with the vision of something that is not real. Therefore, to disillusion someone is to cure them of a belief in an illusion. Gradgrind was under the illusion that Tom was responsible, when in fact it was his sister!

   To transgress is to do something wrong. A transgression is sort of like a sin.
7. To be an instigator is to be the person initiating or starting something.
8. To chastise someone is to tell them off.

   To condemn something is basically to announce that you do not agree or support it or what it has done.

   Compunction is another word for guilt.
9. To be incredulous is to be so surprised by something that you can hardly believe it.

   Pedagogy refers to the way someone is taught at school.

Paper Four: Model Answers & Guidance

1. If something is ambiguous, it means it is unclear or uncertain. The provenance of something is where it comes from. I'm saying that the writer creates uncertainty regarding the exact location from which Hollingsworth's unique voice emanates.

   I've also used the word transcendent here. To transcend sort of means: to rise above all earthly things.
2. To do something with gusto means to do something with lot of energy.
3. If someone is self-righteous, it means that they consider themselves to be morally superior to others.
4. Being sanctimonious is similar to being self-righteous. It means that you are someone who tried hard to show others how morally superior they are.
5. If you describe someone as a figure of pathos, it means that they are an individual who inspires sympathy in others; that is to say, they are a pathetic individual.
6. To galvanise someone is to spur them into taking action.
7. A gate crasher is someone who turns up without an invitation.
8. A voyeur is someone who takes pleasure in watching others.
9. A nomad is someone with no fixed home, and who is thus always on the move.

Paper Five: Model Answers & Guidance

1. An oxymoron is a phrase that combines two contradictory ideas. A famous one is spoken by Shakespeare's Romeo: 'O loving hate!' The ideas of love and hate are contradictory, hence this is an oxymoron.
2. A paradox is when you have two contradictory ideas in tandem (indeed, an oxymoron is a type of paradox – a linguistic one). Another example of a paradox is the idea that God might make a stone so heavy that even he could not move it. The immovability of the stone clashes with the idea of God as an infinitely powerful being.
3. Kinesis means movement. As a result, a kinetic verb is a verb that relates to movement.
4. The phrase Newtonian refers to ideas derived from the works from Sir Isaac Newton - a seventeenth/eighteenth century physicist & mathematician whose work is key to human kind's understanding of how the physics of our universe works.
5. Cadaverous is an adjective taken from the word cadaver, which is a synonym for a dead body. In other words, if someone is cadaverous, it means they resemble a dead body.

6. A taboo is something that society thinks should not be said or done.

Paper Six: Model Answers & Guidance

1. To allude to something is to refer to it.
2. If something is disembodied, it means it is separated from a body. At times, this hand/arm almost seems to be floating and attached to nothing.

Paper Seven: Model Answers & Guidance

1. The etymology of a word is where that word comes from. For instance, a lot of words in English have Latin etymology, which means that they are adapted from words from the Latin language.
2. If something is an anachronism, it means that it belongs to a different time period – for instance, a top hat.
3. A patriarchy is a society ruled by men. A patriarchal figure is therefore a man in a position of power.
4. The word redacted means that it has been removed. In the opening paragraph of the extract, you'll notice that the year is quoted as '18--'. This was a technique used by writers to make their story seem more realistic: they were pretending that, to protect the true identity of the characters who appear in the story, they are withholding the exact year in which it took place.
5. If you are notorious, it means you are famous, but for the wrong reasons!

Paper Eight: Model Answers & Guidance

1. An ictus is when there is a stress on a syllable. Let me explain.

   Think of the word 'donkey.' It has two syllables – don | key. However, when you say it, you say the don with more emphasis, and the key more softly. As a result, we would say the ictus is on the first syllable.

   So, back to the word 'slatternly.' It contains three syllables – sla | ttern | ly. However, we only have an emphasis (ictus) on the 'slat,' which makes it sounds almost as if you are trailing off when you say it.

   In short, talking about stresses on syllables is quite a nice way of going a step beyond pointing out something like alliteration (see footnote number -----). You by no means have to do it to score marks, and I certainly would not suggest you go mad with it, but it is not a bad skill to have in your arsenal.

Printed in Great Britain
by Amazon